D1230437

FatherLove

Books by Richard Louv

FatherLove
Childhood's Future
America II

FatherLove

What We Need
What We Seek
What We Must Create

Richard Louv

POCKET BOOKS
New York   London   Toronto   Sydney   Tokyo   Singapore

PUBLIC LIBRARY
EAST ORANGE, NEW JERSEY

306.87
L894
cop.1

*To the memory of my father and mother
and for my sons*

POCKET BOOKS, a division of Simon & Schuster Inc.
1230 Avenue of the Americas, New York, NY 10020

Copyright © 1993 by Richard Louv

All rights reserved, including the right to reproduce
this book or portions thereof in any form whatsoever.
For information address Pocket Books, 1230 Avenue
of the Americas, New York, NY 10020

ISBN: 0-671-79420-5

First Pocket Books hardcover printing July 1993

10 9 8 7 6 5 4 3 2 1

POCKET and colophon are registered trademarks
of Simon & Schuster Inc.

Printed in the U.S.A.

The author is grateful for permission to reprint material from the following sources: Excerpt from "Two Faces of Fatherhood," by Paul Taylor, June 16, 1991, *The Washington Post*, reprinted with permission. Excerpt from "The American Family, 1992," by Myron Magnet, reprinted with permission from *Fortune*, August 10, 1992. Excerpt from "Not All Men Are Sly Foxes," by Armin A. Brott, reprinted from *Newsweek*, June 1, 1992, with permission from the author. Excerpt from "Life Without Father," by Nina J. Easton, reprinted from *Los Angeles Times Magazine*, June 14, 1992, with permission from the author. Excerpt from "Life Sentence: the politics of housework," by Debbie Taylor, March 1988, reprinted with permission from *New Internationalist*. Excerpts from *Absent Fathers, Lost Sons*, by Guy Corneau, © 1991, reprinted by arrangement with Shambhala Publications, Inc., 300 Massachusetts Avenue, Boston, MA 02115. Excerpt from "Angry Young Men," by Barbara Ehrenreich, from *New York Woman*, © 1989, reprinted with permission from the author. Excerpts reprinted with permission of The Free Press, a Division of Macmillan, Inc. from *FINDING OUR FATHERS: The Unfinished Business of Manhood*, by Samuel Osherson. © 1986 by Samuel Osherson. Excerpts from "Fathering the Nest," *M*, May 1992, 66–75, by Aaron Latham, reprinted with permission from the author. Excerpt from "Why children need both their parents," by Charles Donovan, *The San Diego Union-Tribune*, August 2, 1992, Opinion Page, reprinted with permission from the author. Excerpt from "Dads Who Shaped Up A School," by Hank Whittemore, *Parade*, September 22, 1992, 20–22, reprinted with permission from the author and reprinted with permission from *Parade*, © 1992.

Some of the names in this book have been changed.

Contents

vii

Contents

Part Three

Conclusion

Acknowledgments

Many people and organizations shared in the parenting of this book. its midwife and editor, Judith Regan, ushered it to life. Among those to whom I owe special gratitude are my wife, Kathy Frederick Louv, and my sons, who nurture my fatherhood. Marie Anderson offers daily counsel, wisdom, and a sense of perspective. Jane Clifford, a talented editor, gave up many hours of her family time to help shape these chapters. My friend Peter Kaye helped shape it in ways that he may not know. David Boe and Jon Funabiki and Bill Stothers listened. Karin Winner, Gerald Warren, and *The San Diego Union-Tribune* offered an ongoing womb for the ideas expressed here; some of the notions and tales were tried out first in my column for that newspaper. I am also grateful to Ann Pleshette Murphy and Alix Finkelstein, of *Parents* magazine. John Muncie was an excellent coach and pretty good fisherman. Among the many others to whom I am indebted: my brother, Mike Louv, my agent, David Vigliano; Ron Zappone, Richard Larimore, Dick and Suzanne Thompson, Ellen Kleiner, Ralph Keyes, Randy Wright, Charles Harrington Elster, Patricia Chryst, Ellen Duris, David Mollering, Leigh Fenly, Maribeth Mellin, Treacy Lau, Scott Reed, Viviane Warren, Jackie Green, Jack

Acknowledgments

Levine, Gabriela Schwartz, Danelle McCafferty, Barbara and Ralph Whitehead, Rosalie Streett and Parent Action; the *Union-Tribune* librarians, especially Anne Magill; the Unitarian Co-operative Preschool, and other organizations that helped arrange interviews with parents and children. I am grateful to the academic internship program at the University of California, San Diego, and for the invaluable help provided by Jim Gratiot and Corinne Grimm. And my thanks to Pete Sebring for a suggestion he made long ago.

Introduction

Your child can say something to you, just one small thing, and suddenly the universe expands.

One evening not long ago, I walked with my son Matthew to the library and back. He is about to turn five. He wears small, round glasses. He is an impatient person, eager to cut to the chase, a detector of dissembling.

He is beginning to connect the dots of the universe.

"Look, Dad," he said, "the moon is a sliver."

We were on a nighttime adventure, a four-year-old's favorite kind of adventure. Walking alone at night with your child is when the truth comes out, like the stars.

"Dad, the moon is really the sun, and it's out all the time," he announced with authority.

I stopped and looked up. I explained to him that the moon was not the sun but was lit by the sun, which is . . . look behind those trees, just over the dark horizon, where we cannot see the sun because the world is curved and round.

In the dark, I could feel that Matthew's eyes were big. His breathing had changed. Two crescents of light were reflected in his glasses.

He seemed to accept this version of reality. We walked on for a while, carrying our bags of books.

"Look, Dad, the stars are out."

"Yes, they are."

"Um . . . Dad . . . I want to tell you something."

"What, Matthew?"

"The stars are following us."

And they were. We moved, they moved. I had not noticed or remembered this phenomenon since I was a child.

In his small voice, Matthew said, "The stars are watching us . . ."

"Yes."

". . . and, Dad," he explained, "the stars are fairies."

I did not offer an alternative explanation. His was better than any I could muster. He had cut me loose from the earth.

I wonder if fathers in any other time kept track of what their children taught them, of these moments.

Our culture has little patience with fathers who dote too much on moments. Publishers market memory books, in pastels, to moms: This is when the baby was born; these were my first thoughts; this is when the baby took his or her first step, and this is how I felt in my heart. It seems to be the province of mothers to keep the scrapbooks and records.

True, I bought a video camera. But like most fathers, I prefer to stay behind the lens, and that is where I usually end up.

A few months after my father's death, as a kind of lone late-night wake, I pulled out a box of eight-millimeter films. I opened the box and could smell his cigarette smoke. I gingerly removed the gray metal canisters and spooled the film onto the projector, one of his prized possessions.

Clear images moved across the wall: my dog bounding across time; my irritated little brother waving toilet paper; the morning light filling the kitchen; passing clouds carrying the embryos of tornadoes.

All these small moments. My young mother smiling and waving her hand in frustration; my elderly aunt's lumbering Chrysler; my grandmother in the black, lacy dress favored by older women of that time; a friend and I, both seven, carrying a flag through a field of brittle cornstalks, moving away until only the flag could be seen like the sail of a ship heading out to sea.

In all of this footage, I never saw my father.

Only once was there a glimpse, during a backyard picnic as the Missouri wind caught paper plates and Aunt Mary's hairpiece. There, on the concrete wall of the walk-out basement, behind my mother and brother, was the shadow. It was the shape of a man who still had his hair, a silhouetted pompadour. The shadow was holding a camera.

I wish I could see him in these movies. I wish I could see him.

In the brief years of my own fatherhood, I have realized that when I am fathering I feel more like a man than at any other time in my life. To say this is not to presume that I am satisfied with my fathering; we live in an age when many men sense that fatherhood can be the most mysterious and fulfilling journey that a man can make—but we find ourselves struggling to define the terms, feeling somehow that we have yet to find the essence of our fatherhood or our manhood. Paradoxically, this is also an era in which fatherlessness—the emotional or physical absence of fathers—may be the most dangerous social reality of our time.

Our culture isn't much help; it suffers a kind of paternal amnesia, a masculine stumble. It seems to have forgotten the importance of fathering and to have divorced manhood from fatherhood. To describe the role of fathers, our language—our social code—seems frozen, impotent. As a result, too many men, and women too, view fatherhood as a burden, a list of chores and vague expectations, a paycheck, a child support payment. The issue should be cast more carefully. Fatherlessness itself is not the main problem; the problem is the loss of fatherlove. I have come to think of fatherlove as a kind of ingredient in the society, a vanishing resource, a lost chemical, an essence.

Fatherlove represents the fulfillment, the completeness of masculinity, and ultimately the transcendence of gender. It is an elliptical elixir: fatherlove = lovefather. What we give, we receive; what we receive, we give to the future.

Fatherlove can be offered by any man, regardless of his age, whether or not he is married, whether or not he has custody of his children, whether or not he had children at all. Fatherlove can be infused into the home, the workplace, the community, time, and the spirit.

Until quite recently, relatively little scrutiny has been given to fathering. Among citations on parenting in the University of California's library, there are 136 mentions of motherhood and only 22 of fatherhood. When attention is paid, it usually focuses on the pathologies: fathers who inseminate and run, deadbeat or abusive dads. These are important issues, but society's definitions and expectations of fathers have not always been so low or so limiting.

In colonial America, for example, men were expected to

fulfill well-defined, important domestic roles in the lives of their children. Fathers were responsible for their children's moral and spiritual upbringing; fathers were responsible for their children's education. They introduced their children (the emphasis was, unfortunately, too much on boys) into the world of work and adults. Children often worked and played in close proximity to their working fathers, on farms or in stores. But the Industrial Revolution stripped away this intimacy; fathers left their farms and stores, left their homes to work in factories and later in offices. Mothers assumed many of the duties for which fathers were once responsible. Increasingly, fatherhood became an abstraction.

In postindustrial America, men and women are being reunited in the work force, but they now struggle to balance their work with children, home, and community. We have seen frightening increases in rates of teenage suicide, pregnancy, and child poverty; plummeting test scores and slipping national economic competitiveness. We have looked around for someone to blame: first, it was teachers and schools; it must be their fault. Then working mothers became the target; it must be their fault. Then single mothers; it must be their fault. Now, we're moving on to fathers.

The trouble with this pattern of blame is two-fold. First, there is plenty of blame to go around: What about the culpability of our companies and how they treat families; what about our neighborhoods, our urban planners, our political process? Second, blame and guilt will change nothing. Understanding, compassion, and communication will help, but only in the context of a culture that sees fatherhood as both a gift and a reward. In order to improve the status of fatherhood, in order to make it as important to the culture as motherhood, we must change our perceptions—and that begins at the individual level, with you, with me, with our children.

This book explores how as a culture and as individuals, we can view fatherhood as the most mysterious and potentially fulfilling journey a man can make.

Instead of asking: What do fathers do? this book asks: Who can fathers become? And how can we find and express fatherlove?

As part of the research for this book, I interviewed parents and children and met with groups of mothers or fathers around the country. (Some of the names have been changed.) Most of the fathers who participated in these conversations do not belong to formal men's support groups, and most had never met.

Early on in my research, I met with a group of fathers who work at their children's preschool; it is a co-op, and they are required to spend a few hours a month working there. One father said, "When I co-op, I feel more *three-dimensional* as a father."

What did that mean? I wondered.

"My daughter comes home and talks about her relationship with this child or that child, and they're not just names to me," he explained. "I know these kids. I know the kids' personalities. I know the parents. Knowing these things gives me something almost impossible to describe, a whole set of connections to a world I wouldn't otherwise have."

What he and the other men in the group enthusiastically went on to describe was a dimension of fathering that extended beyond the home, beyond the definition of what is usually considered nurturing.

From interviews with fathers and mothers (and also children) across the country, I have identified five dimensions of fatherlove. Each dimension leads naturally to the next, but not all were created equal. For example, not everyone needs to be a breadwinner or community builder: but every father should be a nurturer.

• First Dimension: Breadwinning.

This is the baseline. This is what the culture tells men they must do, at all costs. Even if their wives earn more income than they do, most men believe at some level that they are, that they must be, the breadwinners. However limiting this dimension is for men, most feel that a man who is not a breadwinner is nothing as a father. Even teenage dads in Baltimore's inner city know that breadwinning is the baseline, so they sell drugs to pay their child support in order to stay out of jail, but of course, by selling drugs, they end up in jail. It's important to be a good breadwinner. But how many emotionally absent fathers have been damned, at their funerals, with faint praise? *He was a good provider.*

Despite the limitations of this dimension, breadwinning can be deepened by those men who have the courage to transform company cultures and change the relationship between work and home. Later in this book, some men describe how they have done just that.

• Second Dimension: Nurturing.

As long as fathers have been around, there have been good, nurturing fathers; but during the 1970s, the nurturing father came into cultural vogue. As mothers moved into the work force, fathers were expected to take on some traditionally feminine duties and attitudes. Nurturing was defined primarily as domestic duties: sharing the daily care of children, reading to them, bathing them, making dinner, doing the dishes, picking up the socks. The men I've interviewed describe these aspects of domestic life that, in some ways, mirror the frustrations of working women. Men find themselves treating their children like walking chore-lists. The depth of the nurturing dimension often gets lost in the rush.

A father's experience of these first two dimensions tends to become chore-based, breathless, somewhat flat. Working women often feel the same way about their breadwinning and nurturing hours; the difference between working men and working women is that women have a fresher historical and biological memory that there is more to parenting than feeling exhausted from working and doing chores. And the topic of the conflicted working mother is widely discussed in the media and among parents, but the conflicted working father is rarely, if ever, discussed. In fact, there's not much discussion in the society about any of the possibilities of fatherhood past, say, dimension one-and-a-half. Even when fathers stick around, that's where most of them get stuck—at one-and-a-half. Fathers, whether married, single, or divorced, say they hunger for something beyond today's limited definition of fatherhood, yet they have no language to describe it.

Fathers are hungry for more than the often chore-based first and second dimensions; the first two dimensions can be deepened through an infusion of fatherlove.

• Third Dimension: Community Building.

When fathers enter the third dimension, they enter the community of children and the community of parents. They move out into their neighborhoods to become involved, to make a better life for their children—to weave the new web of support that I described in *Childhood's Future*. Real men fight to change the environment of childhood, and real men change company cultures—they work to improve company policies toward motherhood and fatherhood. Some examples of the third dimension mentioned by men: co-oping at your child's day-care center; taking time off to volunteer in your child's school; creating a community of fathers who support one another; introducing your child to the world of work; and working in your community for better treatment of children and families, taking your child with you as you do it. In this dimension men begin to feel a sense of power in fathering that they may have lacked.

As fathers I interviewed discussed the first two dimensions, their body language bespoke fatigue; when they talked about the third dimension, their body language changed dramatically. They began to speak excitedly; they expressed a sense of rediscovered or potential power in a nearly abandoned arena, a sense of (if you will) masculinity, of being explorers, change-agents, fuller men. It seemed to me, listening to them, that if the first two dimensions were to have fuller meaning, men must move into the third—must be *energized* by the third. A fatigued person often believes that running, intense exercise, is the last thing he or she wants to do, although that is exactly what is most likely to revive the body. Similarly, a man who feels beaten down by the demands of work and caring for the daily needs of his children can become refreshed and invigorated by moving into the third dimension. That is what fathers told me, although most said they had never discussed this aspect of fathering before. (Moving into the third dimension lacks meaning, however, if the nurturing dimension is ignored.)

- ## Fourth Dimension: Finding Our Place in Time.

This dimension is more difficult to pin down. A number of fathers talked to me about their yearning to find some meaning in their place in time, in their connection to their own fathers and their children and, eventually, their grandchildren and beyond. One father spoke movingly of how, as his children have recently left the nest, he has realized "that I want to be a father until the day I die." A grandfather next to him assured him that this is, in fact, possible. I realized, as they spoke, the sense of unspoken grief that I carry—the subconscious dread that when my two boys reach their teens, they will be gone from me and I will no longer be a father. For I, too, want to be a father until the day I die; I want to find my place in time. In talking about time, fathers describe their yearning to be grandfathers, to develop a sense of what Erik Erikson called "generativity," the final stage of becoming an adult.

- ## Fifth Dimension: The Spiritual Life of Fathers.

Men and women seldom discuss the fifth dimension of fatherhood, but it is perhaps the most important. In Chapter Seven, fathers of various faiths—some of them religious teachers—discuss how men can find a deeper spiritual connection with their families, their communities, and within themselves.

When men do begin to speak of this deeper masculinity, particularly the mysterious third, fourth, and fifth dimensions, they become increasingly excited. They seem more alive. Suddenly fatherhood is seen as the ultimate gift to a man—and to children—a way to fulfill one's life even beyond the time when our children leave home; by viewing fatherhood as a journey toward full manhood, fathers come home. They become fathermen.

FatherLove

The final chapter, "Fatherkeeping," focuses on how the workplace, government, and other institutions can nurture fatherhood. In order to reverse the trends of fatherlessness, legislation is needed, but something more profound is demanded: The cultural silence about fatherhood must end; and the muttered language of blame, guilt, and neglect must be replaced with a poetry of reward and depth.

One morning before I began to write, I took Matthew out to the edge of the canyon behind our home. We sat there in the early morning light, the cool air moving up out of the narrow canyon, listening to the birds. Across the canyon, a cat moved slowly up through the grass.

The next day Matthew would be five years old. In two months his brother, Jason, bright and loving, would be eleven.

Matthew and I sat on the edge of the rock wall, and I hugged him, my last four-year-old.

"You are my four-year-old today," I said.

He hugged me back, arms around my neck. He is usually affectionate, but he is also usually more wiggly than he was that morning.

Just a couple of years ago, we sat on the edge of the canyon with his first pair of glasses, and I pointed to cats climbing through the grass and birds flying, and his eyes were wide because he had never seen these things clearly. His glasses opened the world for him. To me, that moment will also be connected forever to my older son's birth, when I took Jason in my arms to a window and showed him his first day.

Working on this book has been difficult in ways that I cannot fully articulate—ways that have to do with my own father and what became of him and also because this is a painful subject for many of the fathers I have interviewed: When they talked of their fathers, their own fathering came into focus, like this canyon seen through Matthew's glasses.

One evening my wife and I were sitting in the bathtub, talking. I told her that so much of what I am learning about fatherhood suggests to me that my own fathering does not measure up; this book itself is taking my time away from my sons.

"Are you trying to describe the perfect father?" she asked, the steam rising around us.

Good question. Excellent question.

Venturing into the dimensions of fatherhood and manhood is a journey with few landmarks. And a perfect journey is no journey at all.

"You have prickles," said Matthew, rubbing his hand against my chin.

"Yes."

"They're sharp."

Tomorrow his hand will be the hand of a five-year-old, and someday, perhaps, it will be the hand of a father.

Part One

FatherLove
Lost and Found

I

Real Men

IN A COUNSELOR'S OFFICE AT A WISCONSIN HIGH SCHOOL, A group of young women, grades nine through twelve, bump and rustle and laugh and slide their books across the tables. They sit at their usual stations, on a frayed, overstuffed couch, on wooden school chairs, and up on a banquet table.

They're participating in a dropout prevention program in this relatively new and clean, and generally upper-middle-class, suburban Milwaukee school. These girls meet once a week in a small group and talk about their lives. Today, I have been invited to ask the questions. I begin with what I assume will sound to them like a strange question, but I ask it anyway: Are your fathers real men?

There's a long pause, then laughter. "I should *hope* so," says one of the girls.

"No," says a young woman named Jamie. She says this seemingly without emotion. Her blond, wispy hair is piled high on her head. She wears bright red lipstick, a tight black skirt.

Other young women begin to speak. One says that her father has barely said a word to her for two years. Another says that after her parents' divorce, her father "had the right to see me every other weekend, and stopped it, without explaining why." She did not see her father for ten years, and then one day he showed up at school. "I saw him for about fifteen minutes. All he said was 'Sorry,' and then he left again."

Several of these young women are struggling with drug or alcohol use; all of them are being counseled to stay in school.

Later, these girls' counselor, who has been working with troubled kids for over a decade, says their stories are typical of the ones he hears from potential dropouts. But each year he hears more stories like these, told by other students not so near the edge, particularly from the overachievers, the brittle students most eager to please.

In the group today, the young women speak of their mothers, too, but then their voices circle back around, fluttering and diving, to their fathers. One girl, Linda, describes how her father goes camping with his friends and lets her tag along, how "his money goes for his cars, his snowmobiles, his motorcycles. Everything for him, but when me or my mom or my brothers need something, it's like pulling teeth." As she says this, she does not stop smiling.

Another student tells how her father, the first time he got visitation rights, kidnapped her and took her "camping" for a couple of months. She was five years old, then. He's still in and out of her life. "Sometimes he'll call out of the blue. He's a truck driver. He'll call and say, 'Do you want to go out for a run?" And I'll say yes, because I want to see my dad."

FatherLove

Pressed to describe why they consider their fathers real men, the best explanation one of the girls can come up with is: "I don't know, 'cause he works to support his family, and, I mean, he doesn't like, take off work." She says she knows her dad cares about her and her brothers, but the only time he tells her is when he's drunk or high.

They talk about child support, which they consider evidence of love or at least a poor substitute.

"A lot of time he expects respect, but he doesn't give you respect," says Jamie, pushing back a wisp of blond hair. "I tell him, 'Pay your child support like you're supposed to, and tell me that you love me sometimes.' He owes me over thirteen thousand in child support. I turned him in. My dad hated me for that. He used to call me from the jail at night and cut me down."

Jamie becomes more animated. "He's this big Harley guy that everybody's afraid of, but he's the best guy, when he's not drunk. I don't know whether he loves me or not. I want him to so bad. I don't want to chase him, I don't even want the money. All I want is his love." Jamie tells how sometimes her father thinks that he can get out of paying just by "loving me a little, giving me a hug, taking me somewhere." Then she feels guilty for turning him in. "I've already sent him to jail three times. They let him out to earn the money to pay me and my mom. But he doesn't pay."

Jamie's voice grows quiet. "My mom kind of gave up. She's a nurse; she's working sixty hours a week. I don't see her for days at a time. She leaves for work at two o'clock in the afternoon, and I'm home at three. She gets home at one or two in the morning, and then she's asleep. Sometimes I'll just go in her room and watch her sleep, because I haven't seen my mom."

Linda turns to Jamie and tells her maybe she is lucky

that her dad isn't around. "I got put in school detention for swearing at a teacher," says Linda. "I went home late that day, I walked in the door, I didn't even put my things down, and he came after me. He was high, and his eyes were red. I thought he was going to kill me. I was really scared. He beat me up so bad, my lip was cut open. He punched me in the face, slammed my head against the door, and just beat the shit out of me for like, half an hour."

Linda begins to cry, her sweetness pushed aside by rage. "Then I went in my room after he was done, and my mom came home and asked me what happened. I said, like, *'What do you think?'* Maybe next time my dad will kill me." Linda's voice turns oddly compassionate. "See, his dad used to beat him with a belt when he was younger because he didn't want him to be a screwup. Now he beats me so I won't be a screwup. He's just totally brain-dead to the world. He just doesn't understand anything. I love my dad to death, but I hate him," she adds. "I don't know what I'd do if he died. I'd freak out, because he's my dad." As Linda tells this story, Jamie's body appears rigid.

"But it's not like I worship the ground he walks on or anything," Linda adds. "When he's around, he's around, I don't talk to him. I'm barely ever home. He scares me."

Her voice is filled with longing.

What do these girls look for in the boys they date? What are they like? Are they real men?

Linda begins to talk quickly. "It's really weird, because the guys that I've gone out with, most of them have been more or less like my dad. But I don't take anything from them. I'll yell at them if they do something that makes me mad, I'll tell them what I think. With my dad, I more or less keep my mouth shut. But these guys don't scare me."

The young women begin to talk at once, agreeing that the men they go out with are a lot like their dads. "Like, you guys all know Lennie," says Jamie. One of the girls makes a rude sound. "My dad is just like him except taller." Jamie says her mother was raised by grandparents, "who came straight from Germany, and they always kept their mouths shut real quiet, and my dad was always real loud. So I think I got what I look for in a guy from my dad. But I got keeping my mouth shut from my mom. When I used to go out with these guys, I mean, I was like a total servant. I did anything these guys wanted." The other girls groan.

"I'd do whatever they wanted," Jamie says. "Sometimes I catch myself doing it even now . . . like when I went with Lennie, I was the worst. Lennie's the type to boss you around. I would even give him my paycheck when he told me to. I'd need my paycheck so I could help my mom pay for rent, and I'd give it to him."

One of the girls, Jessica, who has said little throughout the conversation, speaks up. She is, perhaps, the most attractive of the girls. "I'm going out with some *wimpy* guy," she says with a cynical smile. "I'm not looking for someone like my dad. God, no. Kevin is totally different from my dad. He's quiet, and he never yells. He never raises his voice to anybody, and he hardly ever gets mad."

So, I wonder aloud, why does Jessica call Kevin wimpy?

"Because he's really, really skinny. I'm not saying that he just blows in the wind, he's got some muscle, but . . ."

One of the girls laughs and asks Jessica, "Is *Kevin* a real man?"

Jessica hesitates. "Yeah. I guess so."

Throughout the rest of the conversation, Jessica calls Kevin "the wimp."

I ask them: In your mind's eye, when you wake up in the morning, half asleep, and you see this future father of your children, who is he, what's he like?

"Caring. There for the kids."

"He's going to be a good father. I'm going to make him be."

What's a good father?

"He's going to do stuff with his kids. He's not going to run away."

"If things don't work out between me and him, he won't leave the kids. Above all, this sounds totally stupid, but when I have kids, I don't care if he leaves me, as long as he doesn't leave the kids."

After the young women leave the room, the counselor points out that at least the kids in his program have the chance to talk about family issues with someone who can offer them some knowledge of child development, some exposure to an alternative reality. But programs like this are rare, and the ones that do exist rarely focus on the power and potential of fatherhood.

"We talk about motherhood a lot in these sessions, but not fatherhood," says the counselor. "I'm not sure why we don't talk about fatherhood or manhood much. I've been thinking we should change that."

A few minutes later, six young men enter. Unlike the young women, who have been vocal and open, the boys are painfully silent. The pauses are very long.

What's a real man? I ask. What's a good father?

Jimmy, athletic, eager, says, "My father's cool, man."

Is he a good man?

"I guess."

FatherLove

What's a good man?

"Somebody that takes control," one of the boys says.

"I don't know. My dad's an okay guy. He doesn't really listen to my problems or anything at home, but he's there," says Jimmy.

What would you wish him to be?

"I don't know. I wish he kind of paid more attention to what I did and stuff, and gave me his opinion."

How about the rest of you? What's a good father?

Nobody answers.

"Don't deny a child," says Michael, a tough-looking kid. He's slouching down in his chair, fingers resting on the bridge of his nose. "My dad's nobody to me. Whenever company comes over, even his own mother, my dad leaves. I've never once sat down and eaten dinner with him. But we've got pictures of me and my dad, we were real close when I was young. Just like he is with my brother now. I'm scared he's going to do to my little brother what he did all of a sudden to me, he just turned away from me.

"I talked to my aunt last night. She told me why my father always put the blame on me. It's because my mom and dad had to get married because of me."

The counselor asks him if he thinks he's the cause of his parents' problems.

He doesn't answer. His hand moves up to his eyes. Tears fall from behind his hand.

The counselor says softly, "Michael, even though they got pregnant with you, they still had choices."

Michael continues to weep behind his hand, and the group falls silent.

After a while, I ask: What do you guys hear from the girls at your school about what they want in a man and a future father?

One of the young men says, "When girls talk, they talk

among themselves, they don't talk with guys around them. I really don't care to hear what they're saying anyway."

Except for Michael, the boys laugh. I ask them: What's a good dad?

"A person who actually listens to what you're saying. Someone you can talk to about something really important," says Jimmy.

"I don't know," another one says. "I guess somebody who's there to listen to you. Not somebody who just sits there in his chair and watches TV and drinks beer."

One of the boys has been silent. His name is Carl. He has dirty blond hair and a bad complexion. He's leaning back in his chair, head against a blackboard, watching through slitted eyes.

"I'll tell you what a good dad is. He's always spending money, buying toys, and hardly has any time for himself," Carl says, a sarcastic tone in his voice. "If you're a dad, you've got to put up with a little kid, and take him swimming and all that crap. If you're not a father, you can do anything you want. You can stay out until five in the morning, party your ass off—if you're a father you've got to be there and tuck the kid in and tell him bedtime stories at eight-thirty at night."

He laughs. He hasn't moved; he's still leaning against the wall.

Suddenly the counselor asks: Carl, who's in charge in your family?

"I am," he says. His voice is barely audible.

Do you feel responsible for your parents? asks the counselor.

"No." Carl's voice is louder.

Do they take care of you?

"They're always good at Christmastime with all the toys. I'm spoiled rotten." He smiles slyly.

FatherLove

Do you think your father is a real man? the counselor asks.

"He acts like it."

I ask Carl to describe his image of a good man and a good father.

He brightens, still sly, and says, "He's got a storybook in one hand and a bottle of Jack Daniels in the other."

I ask them if they think much about what kind of fathers they will be. A long pause. Someone says, "No."

"It's still a long time away," says Jimmy. I remind this boy that at sixteen he could father a child any day now. "Yeah, but I don't plan on it. I swear I'm not going to have one until I plan on it."

Now Michael, who has recovered his composure, speaks up. "I think about it, 'cause a couple of girls asked me. They say, 'What if I'm pregnant, how are you going to be?' I go, 'I'm going to support my baby.' You know, be there. Not like my dad."

I ask: Do any of you look forward to being dads?

"I think it would be nice to have a kid," says Michael, " 'cause it's like something, you know, that you created, you brought into this world by yourself without the help of anybody else except your wife." He says he's hoping to have kids within the next couple of years. "It's something I think about."

The other boys razz him.

"No, really, I've been thinking about it for a while, ever since my girlfriend and I started talking about it. . . ."

II

FatherLove Lost and Found

RECENTLY, I ASKED A FRIEND, WHO IS A FATHER, THIS QUESTION: What do fathers do?

"As little as they can get away with," he answered.

He said this with the knowing look that men sometimes share when the subject comes up. He is a good father. He was simply describing the way our culture, particularly in the American media, views fathers. For decades our culture has been largely silent, or flippant, on the subject of fatherhood.

In addition, the whole idea of fatherhood has been at least partially disconnected from manhood. "Our heroes have never been daddies," writes Hugh O'Neill in a piece for *Mothering* magazine, adapted from his book, *Daddy Cool*:

Consider the pantheon of manliness—the granite-jawed Randolph Scott, Eastwood, the Duke, Alan Ladd as Shane, the outlaws Bogart and Cagney, the denim cool James Dean, not to mention Springsteen. All the legends have one thing in common: they are entirely undomesticated. Cool is the open road to wherever it leads; Daddy is the station wagon to the swap meet.

The fact is that any fool can be cool when he's well rested, well-groomed, when he makes the decisions about his life. But it takes real sand to be cool when you haven't slept since June, when the Burl Ives version of "Little White Duck" is threatening to drive you mad, when you've just been awakened with a GoBot to the head.[1]

Consider, too, the stories we tell our children. In a *Newsweek* "My Turn" column, Armin A. Brott of Berkeley, California, writes of how children's classics generally portray fathers: "Once in a great while, people complain about Babar's colonialist slant. But I've never heard anyone ask why, after his mother is killed by the evil hunter, Babar is automatically an 'orphan.' Why can he find comfort only in the arms of another female? Why do Arthur's and Celeste's mothers come alone to the city to fetch their children? Don't the fathers care? Do they even have fathers? I need my answers ready for when my daughter asks."

Most children's classics perpetuate the same stereotypes of fathers, perhaps because they were written at a time when mothers were expected to do most of the parenting. But so do many of the newest children's books. Each month Brott's local public library previews over two hundred new children's picture books for children under five. Many of the books consciously take the women characters out of the kitchen and nursery and give them jobs and responsibilities outside the home. Nonetheless, moms are still depicted, for the most part, as the primary caregivers and nurturers of their children.

"Men in these books—if they're shown at all—still come home late after work and participate in the child rearing by bouncing baby around for five minutes before putting the child to bed," according to Brott. In a review of twenty currently popular children's picture books, seven do not mention a parent at all, Brott writes; of the rest, four portray dads as less loving and caring than mothers. "In 'Little Gorilla,' we are told that the little gorilla's 'mother loves him,' and we see Mama gorilla giving her little one a warm hug. On the next page we're also told that his 'father loves him,' but in the illustration, father and son aren't even touching." Of the remaining nine books, six portray mothers as the only parent. Only three of the twenty treat fathers and mothers as equal parenting partners.

Isn't this a reflection of reality? As Brott points out, that explanation is unacceptable. "If children's literature only reflected reality, it would be like prime-time TV, and we'd have books filled with child abusers, wife beaters and criminals. . . . Ignoring men who share equally in raising their children, and continuing to show nothing but part-time or no-time fathers, is only going to create yet another generation of men who have been told since boyhood—albeit subtly—that mothers are the truer parents and that fathers play, at best, a secondary role in the home."[2]

Indeed, even parenting manuals and parenting magazines tend to focus more on the mom than the dad. Until the late 1980s, advertising and television shows, with few exceptions, focused almost exclusively on mothers rather than fathers.

Until recent years, popular culture assumed the connection between mother and love, between motherhood and womanhood (so there has been no need for a word like motherwoman). Our culture currently strains to describe the more complex truths with such awkward phrases as "working mother" (most mothers work whether or not they have careers outside the home). As ungainly as our language has become, in describing women and mothers, we need a similar effort to find new words and symbols for the complexity of manhood and fatherhood.

Linguistics suggest that manhood and fatherhood may never have been all that well connected in the public mind. I asked the philologist Charles Harrington Elster, author of *Is There a Cow In Moscow?* and *There's a Word for It*, if he knew of a word in Western culture connecting fatherhood to manhood. He searched, and two days later called to report his astonishment. He couldn't find one, at least not in the languages that have shaped Western culture, although he said that some words and phrases did nibble around the edges.

"There is an odd and uncommon English word, *fathercraft*. Like woodcraft. That word doesn't say much about manhood, but it's interesting. Then there is the word *paterfamilias*, which refers to the male head of a household. Historically, that was an ancient Roman father, someone who was *sui juris*, his own master, and someone who had *patria potestas*, power over his household. Someone with *patria potestas* could sell his children into slavery. This is not a helpful concept in the 1990s.

"Ah!" Elster continued. "But I did find a phrase that is more positive. It's from Polish: *hart ducha* (pronounced heart DOO-ha), which the philologist Howard Rheingold defines as 'self-mastery in the face of internal and external forces.' " *Hart ducha* is considered primarily a male trait. Someone who has *hart ducha*, according to Rheingold, has gained control of his desires and appetites. He doesn't cower, surrender, or flee, or compromise his rights and independence. He has simple dignity and self-control while performing menial tasks. New immigrants to America who work as laborers by day, study at night, and maintain their dignity—they have *hart ducha*.

But where's the specific link to fatherhood? "There isn't one," said Elster. "But I did find three rare words that might be helpful." *Patrizate*, from Latin, a verb that means to imitate one's father or forebears. And *storge*, a noun from German, which refers to the parental instinct or love that animals can have for their young. "When I saw that word, I realized that men are often criticized for lacking *storge*, but we just assume that women have it." Then there's another odd word, coined over a century ago, that could describe what some women might look for in an ideal husband or father: *boonfellow*, a warm, congenial, and intimate companion. "This word seems to capture the sensitivity that men today are supposed to have," says Elster.

As a father, Elster considers himself a boonfellow with *hart ducha*. He hangs on to his daughter's every word. On his computer he records her burgeoning vocabulary. "You might say I'm doing a narrow sociological study of her verbal development. On her first birthday she knew thirty words, including animal noises—bow wow, moo. Usually a child that age knows eight or ten words. When she hit fifteen months, she was up to seventy-five words. Amazing! I guess I'm just a proud father."

I reminded him that we still had not identified a good word to connect fatherhood and manhood. We'd come close. But no cigar.

"Maybe the culture hasn't invented a word because the word hasn't been needed or demanded, until now," he said. "I guess I'd like to think of myself as *paterfamilias* without the nasty overtones. Before being a father I was a boonfellow. I'm still a boonfellow. I'm trying to learn fathercraft, but that demands adaptations in boon-fellowing."

FatherLove

A few months after I spoke to Elster, I did happen on a word in the *Utne Reader* that comes closer: *husbandry*. Robert Mannis, a psychologist in Frederick, Maryland, writes that the word is derived from a combination of the Old English *husdonda* and the Old Norse word *bua*, "to dwell":

> A husband was a household dweller deeply bonded to his home and land rather than a wanderer or nomad. Husbandry also came to be synonymous with the craft of farming. Man's primary role was thus seen in terms of commitment to wife, children, community, and land. . . . The essence of husbandry is a sense of masculine obligation—generating and maintaining stable relationships to one's immediate family and to the earth itself. At its heart, husbandry reflects a bonding of both family and nature through a clear appreciation of the responsibility inherent in the role of provider, caretaker, and steward.

It would be unlikely and impractical for many of us to literally return to this role, of husband of the soil, but as Mannis writes, the spirit of this relationship can be applied to men today: a renewed sense of pride, "a pride gained in the purposeful care for their families and communities as well as in the stewardship of the earth and the husbanding of its resources. . . . A renaissance of husbandry will help heal the deep spiritual wound men now suffer."[3]

Nonetheless, our language is oddly barren or archaic. We lack the words to describe fatherhood—beyond Deadbeat Dad, the Disneyland Dad, the Vanishing Dad.

This stereotype of the disengaged dad is relatively new. In early American law and custom, fathers bore ultimate responsibility for the care of their children. Well into the eighteenth century, child-rearing manuals were generally addressed to fathers, not mothers. Fathers were responsible for supervising the entry of their children, especially their sons, into the world beyond the home.

"Most importantly, fathers assumed primary responsibility for what was seen as the most essential parental task: the religious and moral education of the young," writes David Blankenhorn, president of the Institute for American Values in New York. He also looks backward in time, in order to look forward to a reconception of fatherhood. Then came the Industrial Revolution, and fathers trudged off to work in the factories. Gradually, women added the fathers' domestic responsibilities to their own. And beginning in the 1830s, child-rearing manuals, redirected toward mothers, began to deplore the father's absence from the home.

During recent decades, the phrases most commonly used to describe good fathers are "good family man" and the "new father." Says Blankenhorn:

> Ponder the three words. 'Good': moral values. 'Family': purposes larger than the self. 'Man': a norm of masculinity. This compliment was once widely heard in our culture, bestowed as a badge of honor to those deserving it. Rough translation: He puts his family first. Yet today, especially within elite culture, who hears the phrase? It sounds antiquated, almost embarrassing. Much of the reason, of course, is the modern gender-role revolution. The 'good family man' carries a lingering connotation of sole breadwinner and head of the family. Modern concerns over the phrase are therefore understandable.[4]

The "new father," as David Blankenhorn asserts, aims at androgyny. The term "suggests that good men are those who eschew many historically masculine traits (such as protecting and providing for wife and children) and cultivate historically feminine traits (such as emotional sensitivity and the nurturance of young children).''

Poet Robert Bly, author of *Iron John*, decries the emergence of "soft males," men he describes as limp and low in self-esteem, overly vulnerable to women and corporations.

Blankenhorn and others see merit in the ideal of the sensitive new father "as a corrective to an older norm." But as a new cultural norm of masculinity, Blankenhorn suspects "that most men, and perhaps most women, find it lacking. It certainly appears to be less attractive to men than many of the anti-family role models now prevalent in our society: the modern cowboy, the sexual adventurer, the careerist obsessed with marketplace success, the individualist concerned with self-expression, or the romantic loner with little need for emotional entanglements."[5]

The truth, however politically untidy, is that men will not move back into the family until our culture reconnects masculinity and fatherhood, until young men come to see fatherhood, not just paternity, as the fullest expression of manhood. Married, single, or divorced, a man is enlarged by fatherhood: He can become more than the sum of his parts; he can be a nurturer and a warrior, a breadwinner and a domestic worker. He can be a fatherman. He can give fatherlove.

This redefinition and recommitment cannot come too soon.

"When it comes to making a difference in society and really making a change," says researcher Ken Canfield, "fathering will emerge in the nineties as one of the most powerful ways that a man can express himself."

Canfield is the director of the nonprofit National Center

for Fathering, based in Manhattan, Kansas. In 1991 Canfield's center released the results of a national poll on fathering.

I believe Canfield is correct in his long-term assessment of fatherhood, but most of the results of the center's survey, conducted by the Gallup Organization, paint a pessimistic portrait of how Americans feel about fathering:

• More than seven in ten of those surveyed agree that the most significant problem facing American families today is the physical absence of the father from the home.

• Nine in ten agree that fathers need to be more involved in their children's education; 56 percent believe that fathers do not know what it is going on in their children's lives.

• Half of those surveyed agree that fathers are spending less time with their children than did fathers of the previous generation.

Overall, it's more difficult to be a father today than it was twenty years ago, say eight in ten Americans, and they cite lack of time and money as fathers' biggest struggles in 1992, according to a survey by Massachusetts Mutual Life Insurance.[6]

In interviews around the country, I've found that kids often say that they miss their moms—now that most couples are working—but they often see even less of their fathers, even if their fathers live at home. A middle-class student at Hocker Grove Middle School, in Overland Park, Kansas, says, "I see my dad about seven to eight hours per week. My mom and my dad are married, but my dad comes home, and I see him an hour a night. He eats and takes a shower and goes to bed. Then I see him Sunday afternoons, and my mom is always busy." According to a fifteen-year-old girl at Trinity, an exclusive private school in New York City, "My father always saw his mother, and never his father. The same with me because he works till eight o'clock at night and he's always in bed, or he's already left by the time I'm up." And a teenager at a high school in Philadelphia says, "My dad worked at night, and mom worked during the day. I really never saw my dad that much, 'cause he was asleep or at school or something."

Another reason for urgency in redefining fatherhood is the rise of fatherlessness, which emerged as a national issue during the 1992 presidential campaign.

In a now-famous speech in San Francisco, former vice president Dan Quayle connected rioting in Los Angeles with the rise of fatherlessness—and criticized a television show, "Murphy Brown," for glamorizing single motherhood. Ironically, the link to Murphy Brown was apparently lifted from a *Washington Post* opinion piece by Barbara Whitehead, a Democrat. A research associate with the Institute for American Values, Whitehead is one of the country's sanest voices on family values. For years, she has worked to reduce the polarization of the debate.

She believes that conservatives have a lot to teach liberals about the role of personal responsibility in families. At the same time, she says, liberals are correct when they say that too many public institutions, corporations, and politicians have turned their backs on children and parents.

On May 10, 1992, ten days before Dan Quayle gave his speech about the television character Murphy Brown, the *Washington Post* published an opinion piece by Whitehead titled, "What Is Murphy Brown Saying?" In this article she pointed out that "childbirth is a time-tested way to boost ratings, as Lucille Ball proved forty years ago with the birth of Little Ricky. But 'Murphy Brown' will break new ground." The show, she wrote, reflected a dangerous but increasingly popular notion: Fathers are expendable. After

Whitehead's piece appeared, the *Post* published a collection of angry letters attacking it. Columnists Judy Mann and Carl T. Rowan, both liberal, then wrote columns essentially agreeing with Whitehead's position, but in slightly more inflammatory tones. At the same time, the vice president's speech writers were looking for material to beef up the Bush-Quayle plan to make family values the centerpiece of the presidential campaign.

Whitehead has since learned, through contacts with a highly placed member of Quayle's staff, that her article, along with the others about Murphy Brown, was placed in a packet of background material to help the vice president prepare for his May 20 speech in San Francisco.

In her op-ed piece, Whitehead was not out to blame or shame single moms. She did, however, object to the depiction of single motherhood as glamorous. Such a sophisticated, sexy, powerful professional woman as Murphy Brown bears almost no resemblance to most real-life unmarried mothers, who are usually teenagers, desperately poor, and poorly educated. And while Whitehead wrote that the odds are still against the child receiving enough positive parental contact, "This idea plays into powerful male fantasies of sexual freedom and escape from responsibility. . . . Murphy Brown's example encourages an equally powerful fantasy among women. It is the fantasy of the girl left alone to play with her dolls."

She was correct that a TV-dominated culture that encourages these fantasies is in for big trouble. Fathers should not be thrown out with the bathwater. Indeed, the National Commission on Children, chaired by Sen. Jay Rockefeller, a Democrat from West Virginia, worked for two years to hammer out a 1992 bipartisan report that in part emphasized the need to encourage two-parent households—that the best environment for a child is one with a loving mother and a loving father. Quayle repolarized the debate, reclaiming the family values political turf for the right.

"This is a step backward for the country," says White-head. "In recent years, we were finally creating some common ground between liberals and conservatives. We were making progress."

Once again, the issues of family values were politicized and trivialized by politicians and by the media. And the cultural silence about fatherhood continued, as did fatherlessness.

Is America in danger of becoming, in effect, a fatherless society, shorn of its male parents not by war or disease but by choice? A look at the statistics of family life suggests that the answer may be yes. One study suggests that two years after a divorce, more than 80 percent of the noncustodial parents—most of them fathers—have little or no steady pattern of visitation with the children. A second reason for fatherlessness is the rise in out-of-wedlock births. In 1990, 27 percent of all births—more than one in four—were to unmarried women, a fivefold increase in thirty years, according to the Census Bureau. (The rate peaked in the 1970s and has dropped slightly.) The percentage of white children born to single parents has nearly doubled over the last decade, to almost 20 percent. This is a much faster growth rate than that found among black Americans.

At the same time, alternative family forms are increasing in number and variety. Cohabiting couples, for example, have increased from half a million in 1970 to 2.5 million in 1988.[7]

Families today include nuclear families, unmarried heterosexual and homosexual couples, single-parent families, stepfamilies, foster and adoptive families, childless couples, and multiple-adult households. Single-father families are growing at a faster rate than the multitude of other family types. Still, single fathers constitute a demographic blip on the screen. The vast majority of single parents are still mothers.

Today, one in four American children lives in single-parent, usually female-headed, households. More than half can expect to live in such households before they turn eighteen.

About 40 percent of the children who live in fatherless households haven't seen their fathers in at least a year. Of the remaining 60 percent only one in five of these children sleeps even one night a month in the father's home. Only one in six sees a father an average of once or more per week, according to a study by Frank F. Furstenberg, Jr., and Kathleen Mullan Harris, both of the University of Pennsylvania. More than half the children whose fathers don't live with them have never been in the father's home.[8]

Perhaps justifiably, some women now believe that men aren't needed anyway.

"The best thing about being a single mom," one mother says, "is that there's no interference from the other parent in raising the child. You don't have those arguments in the hall—*yes they can, no they can't, why can't they?*"

Many poor women understandably view welfare checks as more reliable than men. Past government policies have, at best, viewed the father as a marginal presence in the family. The nation's social-service system directs its efforts toward helping moms, not dads, who are viewed as the donors of sperm and child support payments, and not much more.

In addition, as more women have become successful in their careers, they have less reason to see men as necessary parenting partners, financially if not emotionally.

FatherLove

With bitter humor, a successful New York career woman refers to her ex-husbands, the fathers of her two children, as Sperm Donor Number One and Sperm Donor Number Two. She says:

> I'm at an advantage because I'm now able to afford a decent apartment and a nanny. I've never received a dollar in child support from Jamie's father. I could have spent a lifetime and a fortune chasing after him in court, because if a man doesn't want to pay, he can get out of it. I can handle not receiving financial support for my son, but watching the devastating heartbreak he feels because his own father doesn't care enough to give him time and love has been the most painful experience of our lives. At so many school events, Jamie would look around the room to see if anyone was there. He would see me, and the other kids' fathers, and I know how profoundly it crushed him that his own father was never there. Never. More than anything I wanted a father for my son. That's why I remarried a man with two sons. But he, too, rejected my son. He wanted to make sure his own children didn't feel that he cared for my son as much as he cared for his own.

She says she has seen men who are nice to kids, but she has (though they certainly exist) never met a successful stepfather. Her current husband, she says, was very nice to Jamie during the courtship, unlike other men, and that is part of what attracted her to him. He promised to adopt Jamie as his son but did not. One time when Jamie was in kindergarten, he made a beautiful invitation to an open house and gave it to his mother's new husband. Jamie said, "Dad, I want you to come." Her husband did not open the invitation. Instead, he looked at Jamie and said, "I don't have time for this shit." The mother says, "I wanted to kill him. What he killed in my five-year-old son was his spirit, his hope, his love. Jamie stopped calling him Dad after that."

Until this year, she tried to match her son with male role models.

You know what I say to this now is *horseshit*. I have a friend, a very powerful media guy, and every now and then he comes and picks up my son. But he watches his watch. I paid a male tutor fifty dollars an hour, I paid a male piano teacher—who was actually wonderful with my son—and I arranged for male teachers in school, though, strangely, he never got along with them. I did this because I was supposed to. But this year his teacher is female, and his adviser is female. My son told me, 'Mom, you know women are so much nicer than men,' and he's right. My son is very macho and athletic; he's not wimpy. But he responds to the females. Here I've been sticking him with all these guys, and he thinks they're a bunch of jerks. Now that his adviser and his teacher are women, he's doing much better. What I've learned is he doesn't need a father substitute. He needs his father. I don't believe women don't need men. But I do believe women should beware of their fantasies. It's lonely and isolating to raise a child without help, but if you marry the wrong man, which is likely, you just end up with more people to take care of and more heartbreak and rejection for your child, which is devastating. If I had it to do over, I never would have gotten married again. I would have stayed on my own.

FatherLove

Divorce and nonmarital birth have lost most of their social stigma. Two-thirds of all mothers are now bringing home a paycheck. Increasingly, fatherhood has become a volunteer commitment.

Jeanne Ambrose, a reporter with *The Grand Rapids Press*, writes that the legal, ethical, and moral implications of helping single women become pregnant keep most West Michigan physicians from artificially inseminating them. "But, the increase in demand from single women for donor sperm, coupled with the fact that women who can afford the procedure tend to be financially responsible, has resulted in lifting the unofficial ban in some parts of the state." In 1991 the University of Michigan's division of reproductive endocrinology adopted what it called "a major policy change." The program began offering donor insemination to single women. Before that, only couples were aided in their efforts to produce a child through artificial insemination or in vitro fertilization. In 1992, of thirty women who came in for anonymous donor inseminations each month, 5 percent were single women.[9]

Maybe dads *aren't* needed anymore.

On the other hand....
I keep thinking of teenagers in Wisconsin who spoke so movingly of their love for their fathers and of the homeless children who create miniature "families," groups of three to ten kids, with the most charismatic becoming the "Dad." Fathers are needed in ways that go beyond logic or social fashion. Fathers are also needed because two paychecks are better than one and because the job market still unfairly favors men.

The following studies show the importance of having more than one parent in the household:

- Most single mothers work full time, but earn no more

39

than $20,000 and receive little child support. A child in a female-headed household is six times more likely to be poor than a child in a two-parent family. The median per capita income for children in single-parent families is less than one-third the median per capita income of those from two-parent families. Two-thirds of single-parent children will fall into poverty before they reach eighteen compared to 20 percent of those from two-parent families. After divorce, children are twice as likely to be poor, according to a Census Bureau study.[10]

• Most research on infant health has focused on the behavior of the expectant mother, according to Louis W. Sullivan, M.D., U.S. Secretary of Health and Human Services. "We are beginning to realize, however, that the behavior of the expectant father is also very important," Sullivan says. "Having the support of a husband may play a larger role in infant health care than factors such as maternal income and educational attainment. For example, the mortality rate of infants born to college educated but unmarried mothers is higher than for infants born to married high school dropouts."[11]

• The most reliable predictor of crime and teenage pregnancy is not income or race, but family structure. Seventy percent of imprisoned U.S. minors have spent at least part of their lives without fathers. Gangs feed on fatherless sons, as Nina J. Easton reports in the *Los Angeles Times Magazine*. She writes: "Father Greg Boyle of Dolores Mission Church in East Los Angeles once listed the names of the first 100 gang members that came to mind and then jotted a family history next to each. All but five were no longer living with their biological fathers—if they ever had."[12]

• The proportion of single-parent households in a community predicts its rates of violent crime and burglary, according to a study published in the *Journal of Research in*

Crime and Delinquency. "Two-parent households provide increased supervision and guardianship not only for their own children and household property but also for general activities in the community," according to researchers Robert Sampson and W. Byron Groves. "From this perspective, the supervision of peer group and gang activity is not simply dependent on one child's family, but on a network of collective family control."[13]

The relationship between crime and fatherlessness is seen in all segments of society, but it is most pronounced in the inner city, where murder is now the leading killer of young men.

"It's not just the absence of a stable adult male figure from a single household that does so much damage in these communities," according to Mercer Sullivan, a research associate at the New School for Social Research in New York. Mercer has been studying the inner city for the past thirty years. "At the neighborhood level, when you have lots of households where fathers are not present, the whole social order breaks down. Teenagers take over the streets."[14]

• Children with fathers at home tend to do better in school, are less prone to depression, and are more successful in relationships. Children from divorced families, especially boys, on average score lower on reading and math tests. Single-parent children are twice as likely to drop out of high school as two-parent children.[15]

• Other long-range studies have shown that elementary school children from divorced families (who usually live with their mothers) are absent more, are more anxious, hostile, and withdrawn, and are less popular with their peers than their classmates from intact families.[16]

• Children from one-parent families (again, usually mothers) achieve less and get into more trouble than children from two-parent homes, according to a study of eighteen thousand students sponsored by the National Association of Elementary School Principals. In fact, children from low-income, two-parent families outperformed students from high-income, single-parent homes.[17] Almost twice as many high achievers come from two-parent homes as one-parent homes, which may simply suggest that two parents have more time to help with homework.[18]

• Children from single-parent homes are as much as 200 percent more likely than children from two-parent families to suffer emotional and behavioral problems, according to a National Center for Health Statistics study. Over 80 percent of adolescents admitted to hospitals for psychiatric reasons come from single-parent families.[19] What about children with stepparents? The financial conditions of these children improve. But according to the National Center for Health Statistics, children with stepparents are at least as likely as children from single-parent families to have learning, emotional, and behavioral problems.[20]

• Compared with adults who have grown up in two-parent households, men from divorced families are 35 percent more likely and women 60 percent more likely to get divorced or separated. Psychologist Judith Wallerstein, co-author of *Second Chances: Men, Women, & Children a Decade after Divorce,* followed the progress of 130 children of divorce fifteen years after the divorce. Many of the boys experienced learning and behavior trouble in school. In their early years, girls did much better emotionally and in school than the boys. (In fact, as other studies have shown, they did even better than girls from intact families.) But Wallerstein found that by the time they became young adults, girls and boys were experiencing equal difficulty forming loving relationships. The girls were fearful of being alone, fearful that men would abandon or betray them. Many of the girls jumped from male to male, married early, and divorced at a high rate. The boys, as they grew up, resisted relationships with girls.[21]

It is true that many of these outcomes would be different if society offered more financial and emotional support to single mothers. But an equally important goal, one that is more important in the long run, is the improvement in the quality of fathering. That focus should come early in how we educate boys—and girls—about fathering; and the focus should be wide, applying to fathers and stepfathers within intact nuclear families or blended families; custodial fathers as well as noncustodial fathers.

Now for the good news, the countertrends.

• Fathers will be viewed as *more* important in the future. A growing body of research suggests the importance of fathers to children's development. Unfortunately, this evidence is coming to light mainly "through the discovery of just how much damage uninvolved fathers have done," says Ken Canfield. Increasingly, it won't be enough for a father to be a good financial provider or disciplinarian. Fathers will be expected to be more involved and nurturing. Much of the pressure for this change will come from working women and women who grew up without fathers in their homes. Men will face what amounts to a revolution in rising expectations.

• The medical profession now considers fathers to be important participants in the birth process. Some hospitals even offer counseling for *male* postpartum depression. Presumably, a father's presence at birth strengthens his commitment to the fathering task. (Other changes reflect the growing value placed on fathers: some newly constructed public men's rest rooms now feature diaper changing tables.)

• Increasingly, men will view being a good father as a source of good emotional health.

• The role of grandfathers is expanding. Grandfathers increasingly act as a male stop-gap, filling the role of the absent father. As Canfield points out, freedom of travel encourages more frequent visits by grandfathers, who are generally younger, healthier, and busier than previous generations of grandfathers.

• Madison Avenue and Hollywood are beginning to portray fathers as nurturers. In a Dawn detergent commercial, for example, a dad washes dishes with his preschooler. In a Northwestern National Life Insurance Company ad, a father hugs a small child and pirouettes, with no mom in sight. From "The Cosby Show" to "Roseanne," fathers are portrayed quite differently from the way they were just a few years ago; some of these fathers are a far cry from the stoic or pitiful dads in sitcoms of the fifties, sixties, and seventies. Yet, progress in the media is slow.

Just as the culture must recognize the good news about fatherhood, individual fathers must also take stock.

If, as individual men, we were to make a list of what we love about fathering and a list of what frightens or overwhelms us, the positive list would likely be longer than the negative. Why, then, as individuals and a culture, do we spend so much time describing what frightens or overwhelms us, rather than exploring and expanding how our fatherhood nurtures us?

There is no fast formula for what good fathers should do or who they can become. But more men are seeing the wisdom of getting off the fast track and onto the family track, out of the corporate boardroom and into the family room. The good news, the great good news, is that an enormous payoff awaits the culture, and individual men and their families, as men move deeper into the dimensions of fatherhood. That movement has already begun.

Like many fathers, I often feel that I am making my own fatherhood up as I go along. I believe that my father felt the same way, and probably, coming himself from a punitive and harsh family with a history of mental illness, raised by a father who demeaned him, that he had less luck than I have been blessed with. I have only a few images of my father's upbringing, since my father refused to talk much about his past, and after his death, my aunt wrote a long letter to me, telling me that the seeds of his death, and the means of his death, had been planted long before the seeds of my brother and myself. She told me a story: She and my father had been out playing. My aunt had pushed him, and he had fallen. His arm was fractured, but at dinner he sat with his arm below the table, stoic. He feared to show his pain to his father; he did not want to get his sister into trouble. What went on in a family like that? His father later fell into permanent silence; I remember my father's father as an old and bitter man in a rocking chair, gripping a cane, turned inward to darkness. I wonder what *his* father was like.

Fathering has never been easy for any generation, and the difficulties a man has with his fathering are in large part personal—like the family fractures that my father carried—but they are also cultural and generational. For decades now, perhaps longer, the cultural container of fatherhood has squeezed much of the joy out of it.

I spend more time with my children than many fathers I know, but less than others. I often move through Saturday and Sunday fighting a series of exhilarating and painful emotions. I find that I am overwhelmed at times by the noise of my boys, by their demands and my wife's expectations. Often, during these hours, my mind is in a no-child's land between work and home. My wife, who works as a nurse practitioner during the week, experiences many of the same feelings. I find my weekend depressions and evening avoidances at odds with what I *believe* I should be doing.

Most of us, one way or another, attempt to reestablish our families of origin. Consciously or unconsciously, we wish to heal our childhood wounds by making over what cannot be made over.

Often, I dream about moving, with my wife and children, to the lake where I grew up, a place made perfect by my childhood need to escape my father's long, alcoholic weekends. Sometimes I fantasize about going back to the lake and buying the house my father and mother built. In some recessive ventricle of my heart, I am continually taking charge of my family of origin, trying to remake it, paint over it like an old oil painting. Nothing works; this is a fruitless and frustrating endeavor because, of course, it can never be fixed, at least not on that lake, in that time, which is gone. Yet, I doubt that I will ever give up trying.

In my daily life as a father and husband, there is this residue: As a boy, I remember fear and apprehension when my father came home: *I can hear his car crunching up the drive; I must steel myself for whatever can happen, for whatever mood he brings in the front door with him; part of me is glad he is home; most of me is not.*

When I come home, my sons rush out the front door and sometimes hug me. At times, I almost flinch when they do this because I am still surprised, after years of this joy. I find myself feeling, at times, unnatural: *This should not be happening, they should fear me, they should resent me, and I am not really needed here, I should not be here.* I am, in these moments, my father.

But every father who finds himself feeling unnatural or illegitimate in the present must, sooner or later, confront the ghosts who are driving home with him.

Part Two

The Five Dimensions
of Fatherhood

III

The Man Who Divorced His Company

As PRESIDENT OF DESIGN STUDIOS WEST, INC., AN URBAN design and planning firm in Denver, Colorado, Donald Brandes, Jr., forty, had charged headlong through the 1980s, building his firm, following his father's example as a frenetic breadwinner.

But the birth of his son, Andrew, four years ago, was a turning point in Brandes's life. "Andrew was the first person in my life who I couldn't con or convince or impress. My height and my weight and my money and my promise had no effect on him."

That realization fundamentally changed Brandes.

One day he assembled his partners and his small, hard-driving staff and made a little speech to them, about how he was divorcing them. "The most important thing in my

51

life is my family," he said to them. "I am not going to work Saturdays and Sundays and evenings anymore, and I am not going to value employees who work evenings and weekends.

"I will value people who work less and work smarter, who work fast and focused, and spend time with their families or their lovers or their boats, because that's what I am going to do."

He would no longer mentor the younger men in his office, no longer spend so much time attending to their psyches.

He told his partners, "I love Patty and Andrew more than I love you, more than I'll ever love you. Don't expect me to play golf with you, don't expect me to invite you over for dinner or get drunk with you or commiserate with you, because it's going to confuse me."

This was not an easy decision.

Women talk about the biological clock; men talk, indirectly, about the financial clock. Some men and women watch both clocks. For many baby boomers who have children in their thirties and forties, the child-rearing years and the peak earning years overlap. Brandes knew he had only a few years to make his fortune, to make his mark. But in that same period, his son was going to grow up.

His wife did not believe that he could cut back. And Brandes was not sure either.

"I had been through a previous marriage. I was able to use words to tell a human being that I loved her very much but, in fact, I loved my work. I didn't want to lie anymore, didn't want to b.s. about 'quality time' anymore."

He felt that he had to declare his decision to spend more time with his family publicly, like a vow of marriage, in order to make it stick.

The testimonial stunned his staff.

FatherLove

They were embarrassed by it. They were uncomfortable. Some employees worried that the company might fail because its president was going through some kind of bizarre male-hormonal change. Some employees may have thought he was being sanctimonious. But he was not being phony.

The transition took two years, but it took.

"I had to rethink trips. I had to think more strategically about how I worked and how I assigned work. My expectations for people's performance changed dramatically. I wanted people to be prepared for meetings because I was no longer going to extend the day into the evening."

Andy Bush, a partner in the firm, is single. He remembers the resentment that nonparents in the company initially felt toward Brandes. "Suddenly the single employees were taking up the slack of the married employees, who were following Don's lead. Don and the others had remarried their families, but we were still married to the company.

"The upside," says Bush, "is that Don's example made all of us realize how out of balance our lives had become. We may not have kids, but we do have relationships outside DSW. Don's sense of balance comes from being able to go to a soccer game without feeling guilty; mine comes from spending time with friends or going skiing without feeling guilty."

And Bush says DSW became a more productive company as it shifted its focus from the number of hours worked to the quality of those hours.

Looking back, Brandes thinks he may have overstated his case to his employees. "But I was scared, see. I thought: Maybe I'll never be at home, maybe Andrew will never know me," he says. "Looking ahead was like watching a bad movie, and the movie was about myself and my wife and my son. I probably overreacted and scared my employees and was offensive to them. But I don't regret it. To this day, I'm known as the company 'family man.' And that's okay with me."

When men talk about their fathering, the conversation inevitably begins, and often ends, at the first dimension of fatherhood: breadwinning. They see it as both their elemental responsibility and, often, their prison. They talk about their fathers. Some speak with bitterness about how little they saw their own fathers, how work took their fathers away, and how vacations were a poor substitute for daily contact. One father, Stewart, says:

> My dad owned a small business, so he would leave for work at three, four, or five in the morning and would get home at three, four, or five in the afternoon. By eight o'clock, he would be asleep. So he was absent, you know, except he would take these two- or three-week vacations a year. And some of those were just him and my mom going off to Europe, but sometimes it was like a two-week ski vacation with the whole family. So we had really good vacations, but the majority of the time he was just either working or asleep in front of the TV.

Another father, Scott, says that his father never relaxed from his long hours of work as a physician, and that, consequently, his time with his father was often tense:

> We had vacations from hell. I remember a particular vacation, to the Sequoias. The whole time, my dad

was totally pissed off about everything. My sister was at the point where she was crying, I was real stand-offish. That was a typical vacation. One time, my dad volunteered to do a kind of one-on-one with me and become a doctor at the Boy Scout camp. My dad brought this black Ford Fairlane that he absolutely loved. The camp had big drainage gutters for the downpours up in the mountains. My dad drove in, made a left, missed the initial driveway, and his front right wheel slammed into this thing. I think he broke his axle. That was the beginning of the vacation. Looking back, I see vacations with Dad as being pretty stressful. Most of the time was spent watching my mother try to calm my father down.

Scott smiles as he tells this story. He says that, like his father, he finds it difficult to disengage from his work as a community organizer.

For some men grief is mixed with respect and awe. Joe, for example, said that speaking of his father was cathartic, and he spoke of what his father taught him. Joe surprised me. He described his father as an absent father, yet admired his father's work ethic and the fact that the time that he did spend with his father was focused:

I didn't see him a whole lot, and when I did see him he was in bed. I crawled into bed with him; he'd hold me, talk to me.

He was an older man when he had me, and he was very, very wise. He was a factory worker. It would have been nice to have a father—I really wish I'd had that—who was able to play with me, but he was exhausted all the time. But he did impart wisdom to me. He would tell me, "I want you to type me a letter and tell me what you've learned today." Every day. It seemed like I did that for years, type him a letter and tell him what I learned in school. So, as a ten-year-old, I taught myself how to type, to write him the letters. He would tell me, "You can teach yourself anything." That's the way my father was: self-taught. With my grades, they always had to be straight A's, and straight A's weren't good enough. They had to be even better. All those years he was alive, he told me, "You need to get an education. This is the only way you're going to advance. You need to do it. Don't do what some of your friends are doing. You need to study. Go to school until you're thirty years old, then you can begin to enjoy your life." I said, "Thirty years old, you've got to be crazy." When you're ten, thirty years old is like a hundred. But now that I look back, I know he was right.

With our daughter, I talk about it, and I don't know how good a job I'll be able to do, but I'd like to give her some of the wisdom that I learned from my father. I'd like to be a provider of that. I don't want to be a martyr, but I also want to make sure that I meet my responsibility, financially, that the family is provided for. That's what I learned from my dad.

While we may judge men too easily and too harshly for hard work, it is also important to realize how limiting this dimension has become for many fathers. Women are treated as sex objects, but men too often are treated, or treat themselves, as success objects. A San Diego father says:

My internal wiring and all my upbringing and training say that I'm expected to fill the provider role, and I fill that. I want to do that. I think I would still think of myself as the main breadwinner even if my wife made more than I do. I want to go out and be the breadwinner. It's all I know. I'm frightened to death to think of what people might think of me if I wasn't making good money, if I wasn't the main breadwinner of my family.

In Des Moines, Iowa, Lawrence, a minister, told this story of how his father's work ethic (and tough economic times, then and now) shaped him:

I came from a very, very poor family, but then, when my dad got that first job as an air force base mechanic, we thought that was the best thing in the world. Then he became the first black automobile mechanic in Des Moines to have his own shop. He struggled all his life to make something for the family. You know, it hurt me very much because he did all this struggling, and then he said, "This is all I have to offer you." I cried because he didn't have to offer me anything, because he already offered me love when I was growing up and struggling to make ends meet. I keep pushing on to make life better for my family. And my wife keeps pushing on to make it better for us. And even though we can't make the ends meet, we just have to struggle that much harder. Sometimes I feel like I'm failing my family, and it hurts, so I work that much harder, like my dad.

No man or woman wishes his or her breadwinning ability to be demeaned or diminished. A father who hides in his work can damage his relationship with his family. On the other hand, a commitment to the family and the community through hard work can also be an expression of fatherlove. The trick is to find some sense of balance. But let's be realistic. Breadwinning isn't getting any easier.

The vise of economic pressure is tightening on both parents. Throughout the 1980s, families barely held their own economically, and only because women worked longer hours than ever. Nearly half of American workers worry about their jobs and feel pressure to prove their value as a result of the recession, according to a 1991 study by Northwestern National Life Insurance Company. "American companies have become pressure cookers," asserts Peggy Lawless, a researcher for the study. "Overstressed employees are less able to perform their jobs and more afraid to leave them."[22]

At the same time, the cost of raising a child is increasing rapidly: American Demographics estimates that a baby, in its first year of life, costs $5,774, twice as much as thirty years ago, after adjusting for inflation. (The main reason for the increase is day care.) According to the U.S. Department of Agriculture, the total cost of raising a child from birth to age eighteen is about $100,000.[23]

Juliet Schor, in her book *The Overworked American*, shows that the average U.S. employee puts in 163 more hours a year now than in 1970, and more than workers in many other highly industrialized nations.

American women are paying a high price: For every additional hour they have added to their jobs, they have shaved less than half an hour from their labor at home.[24] Still, working mothers could point to some progress in the workplace during the past decade. Women's salaries have not yet caught up with men's, but they're getting there. By 1988, women between the ages of forty and sixty-five earned 60 percent relative to men's earnings, but women between twenty-five and thirty-five earned 78 percent, and young women between the ages of sixteen to twenty-four were earning 90 percent.

Since 1973, real earnings of men between twenty-five and twenty-nine have declined more than 20 percent.[25] Of new workers entering the job force in the next ten years, 64 percent will be women. The number of jobs in manufacturing and agriculture, overwhelmingly male jobs, are declining in numbers and wages. *If* this parity holds over the next decade, men will no longer be able to think of themselves as the main breadwinners.

Most poor Americans are women and children, but in the early 1990s the rate of increase for men living in poverty was higher than for women. Black women today are more likely than black men to have college degrees, and black women have slightly lower unemployment rates. Hispanic women who work full time tend to make more than Hispanic men.[26]

Barbara Ehrenreich, a feminist activist and author of *Fear of Falling: The Inner Life of the Middle Class*, describes the "marginal men" emerging in America's suburbs:

A "way of life," as the cliché goes, is coming to an end, and in its place a mean streak is opening up and swallowing everything in its path. Economists talk about "deindustrialization" and "class polarization." I think of it as the problem of marginal men: They are black and white, Catholic and Pentecostal, rap fans and admirers of pop. What they have in common is that they are going nowhere—nowhere legal, that is.

(Young marginal men, if born twenty years earlier) . . . might have found steady work in decent-paying union jobs, married early, joined the volunteer fire department, and devoted their leisure to lawn maintenance. But the good blue-collar jobs are getting sparser, thanks to "deindustrialization." Much of what's left is likely to be marginal, low-paid work. . . . And there's nowhere for him to put that pride except into the politics of gesture: the macho stance, the 75-mph takeoff down the expressway, and, eventually, maybe, the drawn gun. Jobs are the liberal solution; conservatives would throw in "traditional values." But what the marginal men—from Valley Stream to Bedford-Stuyvesant—need most of all is respect. If they can't find that in work, or in a working-class life-style that is no longer honored, they'll extract it from someone weaker—a girlfriend, a random jogger, a neighbor, perhaps just any girl. They'll find a victim.[27]

Most men are not pushed quite so far, to the economic margins. Nonetheless, they may respond to economic pressure in other ways that are damaging to their families. Men with little economic hope are less likely to marry and more likely, if they do marry, to be marginal husbands and fathers. Other fathers take on a more frenetic work pace, throw themselves even harder into their work, in order to keep up with the economic curve. But the pressure cannot be explained simply by economics. Some of this acceleration of work may be an unconscious effort to stay one step ahead of women, to hold on to their traditional breadwinning status. Or, men may wish to fulfill expectations placed on them long ago—or ones they believe will be placed on them in the future.

A lawyer in New York said he had decided to work harder, in part because of his disappointment with his own father's lack of ambition (and, perhaps, lack of nurturing), but also because of what he assumed his daughters' *future* expectations would be:

A few years ago *The New Yorker* had a cartoon that showed this father and son out fishing. The boy looks at the father and says, "Daddy, where were you when they were making all the big money?" That kind of said it all. There will come a day when my daughter will say, "Gee Dad, it was great you were around and everything, but I need to go to college." One day my daughter asked me, "Daddy, how many people work for you? Who's your boss? Are you the boss for anyone?" I don't want my children to be ashamed of me, so I'm rejecting a whole lot of sixties bullshit that I've been carrying around all these years, that ambition is bad, that you shouldn't want to strive. I latched on to all that rhetoric at the time as an excuse to allow myself to fail, to be lazy. There's a fine line, a very important line, between getting some perspective in your life and using it as an excuse not to achieve something. I don't want to be one of those hard-driving assholes who step on everybody to get what they want, but I also don't want to ignore the fact that I want to be proud of myself. I want my children to be proud of me. In a sense, I suppose that I want children so that I can have someone to be proud of me.

Many of us, as men, share such thoughts and rationalizations. We find ourselves working to please ghosts of the past or spirits of the future. Like many career women, working fathers want it all.

*   *   *

Richard Louv

Over the years, Linda Evangelist and her husband, Joe, intended to set aside money for their sons' college education. Like many high school seniors, the Evangelists' son, Brad, suddenly became aware of the reality of college applications—and the cost of higher education. One day Brad asked his parents how much money they had in the bank for his education. Linda tells this story:

"When he discovered that the bank account was nonexistent," she says, "he displayed the indignation and self-righteous anger that teenagers excel in." Brad was angry at what he considered his parents' fiscal irresponsibility.

"You led me to believe that I could go to any college I chose!" he said to his mother. "And now you tell me there is no bank account?"

Linda is a teacher at Central Union High School in El Centro, California; her husband is athletic director at the school. Their salaries were no match (or seemed to be no match) for "eduflation," the rapid increase of college costs. Currently, four years of education cost between $23,000 for a public institution and as much as $70,000 for a private school, according to the College Board, in New York. This includes the costs of tuition, books, room and board, and other living costs. In 1992–93, undergraduate tuition and fees continued to climb, increasing an average of six to ten percent. Even for affluent families, the prospect of saving so much money can be daunting to the point of paralysis, particularly for parents whose children will enter college years from now.

"We tried to tell our son that we were still willing to do whatever needed to be done in order for him to go to the college of his choice and that he needn't worry about it," says Evangelist. "We had not yet gotten to just how we were going to accomplish this feat, but we didn't tell him that."

Brad did not accept his parents' excuses. "His anger simmered for a long time," Evangelist remembers. "We would literally have the same conversation over and over. 'I can't believe you two didn't have a savings account for my college education!' 'Brad, don't worry about it. We will take care of it. You just continue to get good grades, apply to where you want, and we'll do what we have to do.'"

Eventually, Brad chose West Point and left El Centro for college. But the conversation about college financing changed little, except that now it was carried on over the phone.

"I can't believe you didn't have that bank account."

"Well, it doesn't matter now because the school you chose doesn't charge tuition."

Finally, it became clear to Evangelist that she and Brad were unable to resolve this issue. She needed to come up with different answers, or she and her son would be having the same conversation until he graduated, and perhaps afterward. While he may have seemed ungrateful, as Linda points out, he had been raised to express himself, in a family that communicates. The next time he called and asked the question, she tried a different answer, one that describes the kinds of trade-offs that parents face today.

"Brad, you're right," she said. "We didn't have a big amount of money set aside for your education. Dad didn't work two or three jobs in order to put money into an account. What he did do was coach your Little League teams; go to all your Pop Warner games, always driving a carful of boys; attend all of your school conferences with me. Remember, he was the one who insisted you be tested for GATE (a school district program for gifted and talented students) when the teacher wasn't too enthusiastic and saying, 'Well, I would have to test four or five other students in the class,' and Dad said, 'So, test them all!'

"He encouraged you to play in the band and went to your concerts, made sure that you had the best teachers in high school, and listened to you every time you wanted to talk. You're right. He didn't invest in the bank; he invested in you. He helped create someone that was of such quality that when West Point came looking for potential leaders, you were ready."

When she finished, there was a long pause at the other end of the line, and then Brad said, "Yes, I understand. I'm glad he did it the way he did."

Brad never mentioned the issue again.

"He's home for the holidays now," says Evangelist. "I asked him if he remembered that telephone conversation we had almost four years ago."

"Just barely," he answered her. "But it sounds like something you would say." Brad's teasing answer told Evangelist that his anger had been resolved.

Soon after this conversation, he graduated from West Point. His mother points out that Brad is paying for his education, with five years of service to his country; his older brother earned his way through college on a football scholarship. "Both boys are earning their way."

Things don't work out quite so neatly for many families, but as Evangelist points out, there are different kinds of investments, and different kinds of interest earned; and parents struggle to find the balance.

Fathers feel more conflict between their jobs and their families than many of them will admit to their mates or their bosses or even to themselves. That sense of conflict is increasing. A 1992 survey of parents by Massachusetts Mutual Life revealed money and time as the two greatest pressures facing today's fathers. More than three-fourths mention one of these two factors: making ends meet, 39 percent; and finding quality time for their families, also 39 percent, as the factors that fathers struggle with most today. No other single factor was mentioned by more than 6 percent of the men responding.

Media have been slow to realize the extent of the conflict that many men feel between work and home; this conflict is seen as a working woman's problem.

"You can hardly flip through a magazine without stumbling upon a story about a mother balancing career and family," writes John Byrne Barry in *Mothering* magazine. "And it only takes a spin or two of the channel selector to catch another TV report on the crisis in child care caused by increasing numbers of women in the work force. Where are the daddies in these stories? Do they just mail in their chromosomes between business meetings?"[28]

One reason for this focus is that women are generally more open about the conflicts. For example, in response to an article I had written about the economic pressures felt by parents, I received a letter from a woman who signed her name "J." The letter described the sense of conflict between career and family that many women—and many men, although they may not be open about it—feel.

"Three weeks ago," she wrote, "I thought I was having a serious nervous breakdown (not that I would know one if I had one but something was definitely out of control) and in desperation, I tried to work myself through it. Over a five-day period, I mind-dumped into my Dictaphone to and from work daily." She explained that, like many hard-driving business folk, she listens to a lot of motivational tapes in her car, ones on coping with stress, getting organized, the Supermom syndrome, and on and on. But this time she was the one doing the talking. On the fifth day, she sat down at her computer, transcribed her notes, "and printed out a rough draft of what was happening to me."

Then she spent six hours organizing the notes, which she attached to the letter.

What follows is a summary of the notes:

Between work time and family time there is no time. It is just not working! My work is definitely interfering with my relationship with H (her husband). He is not getting the nurturing that he needs. My kids aren't getting the nurturing they need. I come home irritated, angry, exhausted. My husband only gets the time that is left over after work is done, after the kids' needs are met, household needs are met, essential phone calls returned. Having fun is not a screaming priority. Even when I have time to recreate, I find it difficult to figure out what might be fun. I do not enjoy vacations.

When was the last time I had good sex with H? Oh, a couple of months, years ago! The difficulty in finding time to have sex is compounded by my feelings of inadequacy, guilt about not having it often enough. I feel guilty for having surpassed my husband's financial success. My success is disrupting, demanding, isolating, and stressful. I can't seem to put my needs into words, therefore I can't communicate them to H.

She does not blame her husband. She lists what is right about him: He is always home in the evenings and weekends; he does all the grocery shopping; he keeps the house in repair; he gets fast-food for the family when they need it; he's flexible; he gets baby-sitters. "I am not single-parenting." But she feels that she is letting her kids down.

I want to be with my kids, I don't want to turn around when they are grown and say, "Gosh, when did they grow up?" But by the time I get home from work, I am *wiped slick*. I can barely get the dinner on the table, eat dinner, then I just put it in automatic, get the kids bathed and/or into their pajamas or start laundry, try and make time to sit and read them at least a story (if I don't fall asleep midway) and *boom,* they are off to bed. We don't have quality time, just pressure time. Face it, I only have eight days out of every month to handle all the needs of keeping a household. Face it, my kids are growing up without me! My life feels chaotic and out of control. There is too much to do and never enough time to do it, so I go around feeling that I don't have control and that I'm not working hard enough, and that's why I don't have control.

At work I try to be a very nice employee. I am people-oriented and nurturing. I have an open-door policy. I let other peoples' needs and problems get in the way of my work. I feel like I'm being good when I work; I'll relax later. I don't exercise. I work in the evening, on weekends, and I expect others to do the same. I must keep things perfectly in order. I complete perfectly projects that are of little importance. I am never satisfied with anything I do.

I can't make a mistake. If I say no, I won't get promoted; I'll be seen as a slouch; I'll be making waves. If I don't keep at it all the time, I will lose everything I have gained. What are my options? A four-day work week? Maybe. I can't quit the job, I'm not going to abandon my children, and I'm not voluntarily going to give up my relationship with my husband! I need to establish who is important and what is essential in my life. I don't know who to ask for help or what it would take to quit work, but then again I don't want to quit work and find that I am bored. If I quit, we would definitely be a lot poorer! I feel if I did quit I would be letting my family down financially and letting down people at work who depend on me, who have been good to me. I feel I can't quit my job or go part-time because there is no one to relieve me. There is no one! I feel personally responsible for taking care of them. But at the same time I don't want to let my husband and my kids down.

Millions of people would love to have this woman's problems. And yet, how many cars out there, driven by women or men, are steaming up with such pressure? Speaking into her tape recorder, she seemed afraid to get off this freeway of stress, terrified of pulling over. Doing so, she felt, would cause a chain reaction, a pileup. "I don't want to let anybody down! But it is just not working!"

She ended the tape: "One good thing. I don't have a lot of traffic on the way home from work."

In many of the groups of men I interviewed, fathers spoke, when prodded, with sharpness and sometimes bitterness about their feelings of conflict between work and home. While they did not feel as tugged homeward as did "J"—and admitted that work was often a good place to hide from the more ambiguous realities of being husbands and fathers—they wanted their conflicts known.

"Everybody talks about the conflicted working mom; what about the conflicted working dad?" said one man, in Des Moines. "My wife seems to want something from me, always something more from me. I hear endlessly of her feelings of guilt about working. What about *my* sense of guilt?"

His companions in the group nearly exploded with agreement. They spoke of how guilty they felt for not being at home more, for not being with their kids more, and for not being able to express this in their workplace where, they said, they were afraid that such talk would hurt their chances of promotion or even of keeping their jobs. Don't women feel the same fear in the workplace? "Of course," said one dad, "but they've got someone to talk to about it. They've got each other, they know how to do this better maybe, and they've got *us* to talk to."

I asked this group: Do you ever talk to your wives about your feelings of conflict between work and home?

"Sure, I try," said one father. "But then the conversation almost immediately comes back to *her* conflicts, her feelings that I'm not doing enough at home, and how guilty she feels for working." So, this man said, and the other fathers nodded, he tended to fall into silence. Silence, he said, was more familiar. The way he said this, however, communicated a degree of comfort in that silence.

Another man, Lawrence, said, "The women are looking to the fathers to make it in the workplace. They may say one thing, but that's what they're looking to the fathers for. The mother tends to look more to the day-to-day issues. The father is looking to the big economic picture. He always has that pressure hanging on him, and women don't always understand that. I'm not sure my wife understands that pressure. Instead of explaining it to her, I just keep on working in order to try and make ends meet. After a while, I think worrying about that big picture desensitizes you. The harder you work . . . you come home at night, and you're just numb to everything around you. You just want to shut everything out and close yourself off and relax."

Doesn't your wife feel the same way when she comes home from work?

"Well . . . sure . . ."

Do you ever talk to your wife about the conflict you feel between work and home?

"Yeah, but the conversation always comes back around to her conflicts."

Too often, as men and women, we forget how similar our work-home stresses have become. We could put this shared sense of conflict to work. The first step would be to talk about the stresses more: man to man, man to woman, man to boss. For many men, that would demand a considerable leap of faith, as entrenched as we are in the male mystique of stoic breadwinning and silence. But many women are more invested than they think they are in expecting silence and endurance from men.

The first work that must be done is in our heads. James Levine, director of The Fatherhood Project in New York City, calls fathers' work-family conflict the "invisible dilemma." He maintains that the phrase "working mother" implies conflict, but "working father is a redundancy."

Levine interviews men at major corporations about their conflicts between work and family. He is surprised to find that some corporations are eager to participate in the research, which has turned into a business for Levine. He conducts focus groups on "Daddy Stress" and has trademarked the name.

During the sessions, Levine asks the fathers to divide into teams of two; one father plays the dad and the other plays the mom, or one person plays the dad and another man plays the boss. The subject: How to spend more time with the kids and less time at work. Such role-playing helps the fathers understand their own conflicts as well as the conflicts of others. Among the pointers Levine offers: "Don't say, 'The company's got to cut me a break.' " Say: "I'm committed to this work; you'll be helping me do a better job if I can go to my daughter's soccer games, and of course I'll be taking two hours of work home with me anyway."[29]

*   *   *

FatherLove

Given the current economic transformation, at least three directions are possible for couples. One is for the man to cut back, work part-time outside the home, and to encourage his spouse to take on more of the breadwinning—and fewer of the household chores. A second choice is for the father and the mother to work, but both cut back their hours of work outside the home. A third possibility is that the father and the mother will work in a transformed, more flexible and family-friendly workplace—as they strive to make sure that the homeplace is family-friendly.

Thus far, our culture has viewed changing the workplace as mainly women's work.

Richard B. Stolley, editorial director of Time, Inc. and founding editor of *People* magazine, is the president of the Child Care Action Campaign, an organization that seeks to improve child care within and outside the workplace. In 1991, the *New York Times* reported his efforts and emphasized his uniqueness as a man working for better child care, including within his own company.

"That story struck a nerve," he says. "We got nearly five hundred letters. If I had ever had any doubt that there's a child-care crisis, the letters convinced me. And ninety-nine percent of the letters came from women, saying, 'We're very pleased to see a male doing something like this. Bless you, sir.' But only a handful of letters were from men. Maybe men don't sit down and write letters of this kind. I was stunned by the outpouring of letters and dismayed by the gender breakdown. The message is still not being received by men."

This bias is deep and wide. For example, the debate over fetal protection in the workplace has singled out women. Yet new studies show a strong male link to birth defects, as well as steadily rising male infertility rates that may be connected to the workplace. As one activist notes: Chemicals don't distinguish between a penis and ovaries.[30]

Corporate culture still favors the workaholic, male or female, who puts job before family: One study of working parents showed that 37 percent of all fathers put in more than fifty hours a week. Paternity leave remains so unpopular that the rare man who takes it often gets profiled in the company newsletter.

Several men told me as employees they were afraid to take paternity leave or to even acknowledge their devotion to family. They fear that, like women who end up on the second-tier Mommy Track, they will be treated from that point on by the boss or by fellow workers as second-class employees.

Some dads are choosing the Daddy Track. They decide to put their careers on hold. *American Health* reports that, at one large Minneapolis company, about 60 percent of the fathers under thirty-five say they're not currently bucking for promotions or transfers for family reasons.[31] The trouble is that implicit in the Daddy Track is still the message that parents—fathers—are second-class employees. While many men will choose a less ambitious work path, the paring back of their careers, which has long-term economic implications for families and children, can be minimized if companies adopt flexible, family-friendly policies for all employees.

Father-friendly policies already exist at some progressive companies.

In 1991 the *Monthly Labor Review* surveyed two agencies of the federal government that allowed flex-time. Almost half of the fathers chose this option, electing to come to work earlier so they could leave earlier to spend more time with their families.[32] In 1989, according to the Bureau of Labor Statistics, 20 percent of medium and large companies offered paternity leave. However, few companies encourage workers, particularly men, to seek flexible schedules or family leave. Two of five companies that grant family leave admit that they frown on men who put in for it, according to Catalyst, a New York City research organization.

One San Diego father spoke angrily of his experience. "Try to get time off for family issues or paternity leave in most major corporations or organizations in this country, and it just doesn't happen. I know in my case, I was a manager for a Fortune Five Hundred company. Within the same month, my wife gave birth, my dad died, and, at my dad's funeral, my wife's appendix ruptured. If it hadn't been for the support of my friends and relatives, I wouldn't have made it. Because at the corporation, there was no organizational structure to support me. Their reaction was cold: 'When are you coming back to work? We need you.' Never mind that I had a two-year-old, a wife who was critically ill, and a dead father. A male employee isn't supposed to show any emotions, you're supposed to be tough. You take care of that, and you get back to work. That's how the companies usually think."

Some men resist. The *Wall Street Journal* reports that nearly half of two hundred large-company executives surveyed by Robert Half International say managers aren't as willing to work long hours as they were five years ago.

Today, many men, perhaps even more than women, lie to their bosses, duck and weave and evade, in order to balance work and family. Work/Family Directions, a Boston consulting, management, and research organization, reports that men feel an increasing desire, and pressure from their mates, to share housework and spend time with their children. Male employees experienced a doubling from 1985 to 1988 of work-family conflicts—for example, the difficulty of finding child care during overtime hours.

The *Wall Street Journal* reports:

> In a recent study, one man reported telling his boss
> he had "another meeting" in order to leave the office
> at 6:00 P.M. "I never say it's a meeting with my fam-
> ily," the man said. Another parked his car in the back
> lot to avoid having to pass his boss at 5:30 P.M. while
> leaving for the child-care center. . . . But few men feel
> they can be honest with bosses about family demands,
> says James Levine, director of The Fatherhood Project
> at the Families and Work Institute, a New York non-
> profit research group. "In our society, men are not
> supposed to feel these sorts of conflicts," he says. With
> men facing such pressures, their wives or female part-
> ners are "doubly handicapped: feeling they have to
> 'do it all' and being taken less seriously because of
> their family responsibilities," Mr. Levine says.[33]

This topic came up during a discussion group of fathers
at the Unitarian Co-operative Preschool in San Diego. They
talked about how they felt about taking time off from
work.

Sam, who works in law enforcement, opened the conversation. "Look, let's say the unsayable. If a woman wants
to go home sick because she has feminine problems, we as
a society look at that more comfortably than we do men
going home sick. Like it or not, that's what's the fact, Jack.
The woman can go home sick every now and then because
she has menstrual cramps. A man may have some kind of
health problem and goes home sick for a day or two every
few months, and after a while maybe we might need to
put him on sick leave and get somebody to replace him.
Now, that double standard may change in the future, but
today, we all live it as men, and we know that."

FatherLove

Several men spoke at once, some angrily. Some of the men suggested that what Sam said was sexist; others said it was the sexist reality. Two of the men, who did have flexible working schedules, spoke of how important the flexibility is.

"I got six weeks off work when the baby was born, but I was lucky," said Joe, "Most men wouldn't dream of asking for time off to be home with the kid. I really feel sorry for a society that doesn't make that possible for more men."

Harn, a high school teacher, said that the good thing about working in education was the flexibility, "which occurs primarily because it's a woman-dominated profession." He said he took off some days, even if he was not sick.

"You've gone home?" said Sam. "You've felt comfortable with that?"

"Sure."

"I could never feel comfortable doing that," said Sam. "I have never called in sick. I'm thirty-five now, and I've been working since I graduated college in eighty-one. Never once have I called in sick. I don't fault everybody for it. It's just that male persona indoctrination that I've got."

Someone asked Sam if his father was like that.

"Just like that." Several other men agreed. "My dad would be dying, and he would go into work," said Sam.

"That was the way my father was, too," said Stewart, a labor organizer, "so for myself I won't take off, but for my kids I will. And I'm lucky. I have a lot of flexibility in my schedule. Just last week the preschool called me at work at noon and said that my son had a fever of a hundred and two. So I got a doctor's appointment for two-fifteen, picked him up, and took him to the doctor. My wife, who usually gets home from work around four-thirty or so, came home at three-fifteen. So I was back in the office by three-thirty. Because I have more flexibility in my schedule than she does, my wife and I can work these situations out. I would say that I take off as much or more time than she does to care for the kids if they're sick. But I'd say I'm the only man I know who has that much flexibility."

Men such as Stewart are managing to spend time with their families, rearranging their schedules or making informal arrangements with sympathetic bosses. Informal paternity leave is much more common than formal leave. A 1988 Wellesley College poll of upscale Boston fathers found that 92.7 percent took an average of 5.6 days off when their babies were born, but they rarely took paternity leave, even when it was offered; they used sick days or vacation time.

Some men work late twice a week and quit early one day a week; they switch to the night shift so they can provide child care during the day while their wives work. They talk their bosses into allowing them to work at home, thereby spending more time with their kids.

Among the men and women I have interviewed, this distinction stands out: Men are more likely to favor informal, quiet, surreptitious ways of taking time off; women (who also, with good reason sometimes, cheat the company) are far more interested than men in *formalizing* the arrangements, in changing company policies toward parents.

Fathers are much more likely than mothers to believe that informal arrangements with the company are adequate, possibly because men are still more likely than women to be mentored in a company, to belong to a corporate good 'ol boys network. The receptionist at the front desk, the single mother (or single father) with no power and no connections is unlikely to enjoy such informal flexibility.

In fact, these informal arrangements are, in some cases, disappearing. For example, the *Wall Street Journal* reports that many companies are now taking steps to prevent workers from using telecommuting as a substitute for child care. Fearing the inefficiencies of parenting, Levi Strauss now requires at-home workers to make the same child-care arrangements as they would if they were working in the office.[34]

The demands of the marketplace won't ease up, even as fathers become more committed to the home. Men will find themselves stretched even more between work and family life. Ken Canfield, director of the National Center for Fathering, offers this example: Because of reduced air-line rates for Sunday stay-overs, companies are having their execs fly out early in the weekend, even though their meetings may be scheduled for Monday. Such fathers can no longer count on weekends free for their children. Will they have the courage to push back?

Despite the odds, change is coming to the workplace. Men *will* inevitably push back. One reason is demographic. Though still small in number, single fathers comprise the fastest growing type of households with working parents and children, according to the Bureau of Labor Statistics, even though single working mothers will outnumber single fathers by four to one. Single fathers will feel more of a stake in creating family-friendly policies.[35]

A second reason change is inevitable is because women are pushing companies to adjust their policies toward families. On this issue they are showing more courage than men, at least so far. Time after time, I would ask fathers what they had done recently to change company policy at their own workplaces. Often, men would fall into uncomfortable silences. This was true even among men who had worked out, with their companies, a degree of flexibility for their own family involvements. Why weren't these men working for change in their companies, on behalf of all fathers and mothers? First came the silence, then the rationalizations.

It takes courage to challenge company policies. Fathermen don't whine, at least not for long. They change the company—they infuse it with fatherlove—or they leave it, start their own company, and rewrite the rules.

Here's part of the payoff for finding a better balance between family and work. Aaron Latham, writing in *M* magazine, reports: "A 1991 Wellesley study found that fathers who got along well with their children were insulated from the ups and downs of work and careers. Or, to put it in sociology-speak, being a good father 'buffered men from the negative mental-health effects associated with a poor experience on the job.' If something went wrong at work, they didn't just go nuts."

The Wellesley study also concluded that being a mother, any kind or quality of mother, "moderated" on-the-job "distress" among women. But according to the study, just being a biological father didn't buffer working dads from much of anything. In order for the buffering effect to work, fathers had to be active and involved in parenting.

Rosalind Barnet, head of the Wellesley research team, says there is an additional benefit to being an active father: "The better the quality of your relationship with your children, the fewer physical health problems you experience. Family problems affect a man's health even more than work problems."[36] In tough economic times, good fathers are more likely to remain intact, mentally and physically.

So goes the elliptical elixir of fatherlove.

*   *   *

FatherLove

The 1993 adoption of a national family leave law is an important step in the right direction. But family leave laws, at the federal or state levels, affect only the largest of companies—a minority of employers. Also, family leave provisions help families only at times of childbirth or family emergencies, which for most families take place infrequently. Family leave does not address the daily strains between work and family. Among the needed changes: equal pay for equal work; job sharing; flexible working hours; a provision for employees to work at home; time off to volunteer or visit schools, day-care or elder-care facilities; company assistance with child care; parent and father support groups within companies; and, generally, more time to be family members.

Even if, magically, better corporate family policies are adopted tomorrow, it would be a mistake to assume that our national conversation about fathers and work would or should end. That conversation is not only political but also cultural. Just as fatherhood and manhood must be reunited, work and fatherhood must also be blended. "The love unit most damaged by the Industrial Revolution has been the father-son bond," writes Robert Bly in *Iron John*. As work and home became separated a century ago, boys stopped seeing or understanding the work their fathers did, he argues. Many men, he maintains, adopted their overwhelmed mother's disapproving view of masculinity. Others compensated for their father's absence; they became hypermasculine and violence-prone. Or they fell silent.

Today, Americans believe there has been a decline in fathers' ability to teach children to work: Almost half say fathers are not doing as well on this as fathers have in the past, according to the 1992 study by Massachusetts Mutual Life. But introducing our children to the world of work helps us see work as an extension of our family rather than as an alternate universe, and also helps teach our children about this dimension of their lives. "Work in my own life is a way of teaching," says a San Diego father. "I put the daddy hat on when I walk in the door, but I also put the daddy hat on when I walk out the door. I want to be someone my son looks up to, or someone he emulates."

In Denver I interviewed two men who, in some ways, epitomize the nineteenth century relationship between fathers, children and work. These two men seemed out of the past: Both sported rough boots, black jeans, white shirts, black ties, handlebar mustaches, and neatly combed Wyatt Earp hair. Jay Paul Brown works his ranch near Ignacio, Colorado, as his father did before him, and fulfills his duties as county commissioner near Durango. Cory Sorenson lives in a trailer in Rifle, Colorado. He hangs Sheetrock, as his father did before him. Jay Paul is sure of himself, his eyes very clear. Cory is a big man, a bit hulking and sad; he tells a slow tale, twisted and long, like a strand of DNA, about his relationship with his father. There are pieces missing, parts broken, but it spirals on.

As with many men, talking about work is a way for Jay Paul and Cory to talk about their perceptions of manhood, especially when the subject includes their fathers or their own fathering, and how they include their own children in their work.

Jay Paul said one of the perks of being a rancher is that he can take his children with him when he works. "We work together a lot. I've noticed the two older boys have really started to get more interested in the work that we do, they're asking questions. And they communicate better with me as they get older and as we spend more time together. So many parents don't spend that time with their children. I think when you begin a life together, you need to decide where your priorities are. Are your priorities your children and your wife? Making that decision means doing away with some of the boats and some things that we just can't afford without working twenty-four hours a day.

"For me, it's the time we spend on this land, working or playing or whatever, that makes a difference, more than maybe just nature. I'm sure there's people in the city that have real good family lives. But there's something about just working together shoulder to shoulder, facing your problems together. When we have a crisis at home with the price of sheep or whatever, we work together through that crisis. I think the kids understand, maybe, our family problems more than a lot of kids would, because they're intimately involved. We communicate."

He spoke of this relationship with an ease and comfort I have seldom heard from men in jobs more typical of the twentieth century.

This ease, I learned, came naturally from his experiences with his own father, with whom he had worked as a boy. "My dad, he had a store along with the farm. I worked with him in the grocery store, and then also on the farm we worked together and broke horses, put up hay. Especially in the younger years, and then as I got a little older, he turned a lot of that responsibility over to me. I was always in charge of the livestock; I wanted that responsibility, and he let me have it. It's hard to know if kids learn that today. You learn that responsibility, and that carries right on through to your family, and you feel responsible to your family."

Like any man who has worked with his father, Jay Paul had times of friction with him. "That was normal, for a few years; then, as you get a little older you realize that your dad was smarter than he or you thought he was. The older you get, the smarter he becomes."

Now, he applies his experience working beside his father

to his boys, and he describes moments of magic that he does not feel he would experience if his children were not working beside him.

"May is our lambing time. We'll have as many as two thousand ewes having lambs over a period of seventeen to twenty days. At that time, the whole family works very hard. I used to work this time with my dad and mother. When our kids were small, just starting to walk, they always were with us down at the lambing pens. And they liked to get in with the orphan lambs and just hug them and love them. In the pressure of work, we'd lost track of the children, but then we'd find them in a pen, wrapped up with the lambs, asleep. These times of intense work were hard on them when they were small, hard on all of us, but the kids learned to work and learned the problems that we all have."

Cory Sorenson did not enjoy such a close relationship with his parents as a boy, nor did he then or now experience the relative affluence that Jay Paul does. Nevertheless, when he describes his troubled relationship with his father, it is his working relationship—his side-by-side labor of fatherlove—on which he focuses and which he clearly treasures.

"My dad had a big role in me getting the idea in my head that work's important, that you need to go out there and work for a living. It's good to go out and work. Not only is it healthy, but it's the only way you're going to make it in life.

"I worked with my dad. My dad is a drywaller, too, by trade. He's a finisher. He taught me how to finish drywall. Personally, I like to hang it more because that's where the money's at. But I've worked off and on with my dad. Not always, because we didn't always see eye to eye. He had a lot of different standards than I did, in terms of work.

Everything's got to be perfect, or it doesn't fly with him. I like to go in, work hard, bang it out, get it in and out, and go. He likes to take his time, lay everything out just so. I worked with a lot of other drywallers that said my work's the best they've seen in a long time . . . yet I can work with him, and it's 'nope, nope, nope, tear it down, that won't do.'

"Five or six years ago, working with my father, he hired me to go in and do a job for him. I went in and did it, and after the job was over, we sat around and talked, and I said 'I hope I did you a good job.' He sat down and he told me, 'I've never told you this before, but as far as I'm concerned, you're one of the best Sheetrock hangers there is, and you do a good job when you want to. It's just up to you. When you want to do it, there ain't nobody who can do it any faster, any better than you can.' That kind of stuck with me. It's simple, but it stuck with me."

Here is what Cory's voice and eyes said: His working relationship with his father was the best of what he had with his father, and he holds tight to it.

Thinking later about his words, I remembered the summer when my father arranged for a job for me, as a darkroom aide, in the engineering company for which he worked. It was a difficult time for both of us; his alcohol dependency and his mental illness were progressing, but I can still recall the surprising pride I felt, riding next to him in the Chevrolet on the way to work. I did not work beside him, but I worked in the same building, and as the summer progressed I came to understand, somehow, that he was not entirely the villain that I had supposed; that the difficult relationship between my parents was also shaped by my mother. I suddenly realized that he had a life other than the one at home. My memory tells me that I would have had neither flash of understanding had I not gone to work every morning with him as he drove in silence, through my last summer as a child.

Other men talked of the healing nature of working with children beside them. By their example they demonstrate that involving children in a man's work does not have to remain a rural throwback.

Jon Connor of San Diego describes what he calls his daughter's golden age:

My daughter is ten years old. Seven years ago I was between jobs. I was her day-care provider; her mom worked, and her siblings were in school. I was desperate. I had just finished getting an advanced degree, but I couldn't find a job doing what I wanted to do. I was working as a handyman; I was driving a taxicab; and I was miserable because I wasn't fitting the role of being a breadwinner. But if you listen to my daughter today, she'll sit there and wax poetic about riding around town in Dad's big yellow cab when she was three years old. Or she'll describe the jobs that she went out on with me when I was building fences and painting. Or the time that we were going to take the trolley to Tijuana and we got lost, ending up in Santee, many miles away. It was a great adventure for her. That was the focal point of her young life.

Men's activist Andrew Kimbrall lives in Arlington, Virginia, and works as an environmental lawyer in the District of Columbia. He often brings his children with him to work.

"I bring them into the office, sometimes on weekends, sometimes during the week, and they do small chores around the office. They know who I work with and what I do. They see how the fax machine works, they listen in on client meetings They're twelve and eight. They don't experience separation between who I am at home and who I am at work."

To Kimbrall, taking his children to work is one way he practices being what he calls a "teaching father" rather than a "temperament father"—the temperament father being the kind who comes home grumpy, depressed, fatigued; someone the kids know primarily by his moods rather than by what he knows or does. A friend of his, who recently became a judge, brings his thirteen-year-old son with him to his chambers to help sometimes or just to witness the world of the courts—of prostitutes and criminals and the innocent and the guilty. He tells Kimbrall that his relationship with his son has improved enormously. And, he tells Kimbrall, that he can't believe it took him so long to think of this.

Listening to my fellow fathers, I wonder: What do I wish to teach my own sons about breadwinning? As I sat exhausted after several days of long work hours, my son Jason came into the living room and sat next to me. I asked him a few questions about school. He told me about a comic book he was writing for school, how this thing that he loved—the world of comic books—was suddenly work.

"Boy, will I be glad when I'm done with this thing," he said of the assignment. I told him that it was a good assignment, as long as it did not ruin his love of comics. I told him it was a good lesson to learn, that some projects go on and on and take extraordinary commitment.

He nodded.

I told him I had missed him lately and said I was very proud of him.

And he said, "I'm proud of you, too, Dad."

I assumed that he was saying this because of my work, but perhaps it had nothing to do with work. He knows, though, that I believe work is important. Sometimes it takes me away from family, just as my wife's work sometimes takes her away from family.

Like many of the fathers I have interviewed, I work too hard, take on too much. I moderate my work through the flexibility of being a writer: I often work in an office behind the house. My sons sometimes work a little Macintosh a table away from my big Mac. Or, I sit with a portable computer in the living room. I take comfort in knowing that long hours are offset to some extent by this flexibility, but not enough.

This is what I would like Jason and Matthew to know: to do their best, as adults, to find a balance, to understand that there are times when work dominates home life and there are times when home life dominates work. I want them to know that they should not feel guilty about working hard, particularly if they feel their work has meaning beyond money and perhaps beyond ego.

I also want them, as adults, to have the courage to speak up and change policies for men and women in the workplace. I want them to be able to divorce their work; to know when to quit and come home, and that there is comfort and life at home.

In that moment with my son, I think he let me know, through tone of voice, through something silent that passed between us, that he was glad I was home, that he was proud of my work, and that he understood.

But I'm the adult. I'm the father. I'm the one who must find the balance.

IV

The Man Who Reappeared

WHO SELLS FATHERLOVE? WHO MARKETS IT? WHO SUGGESTS to boys at home or in school that fatherhood contains such dimensions of depth and joy?

In many of my interviews around the country, fathers spoke in vague terms about their impact on their children. They understood that fathering was important, but often they had a difficult time pinning down just what was important about it. Most of them understood that they must nurture their children, but this nurturing was often described as a kind of refrigerator-door list of do's and don'ts, of caretaking chores. When I asked fathers what attributes their paternal nurturing helped shape in their children, they would often struggle for words: Strength? Responsibility? I seldom heard fathers describe empathy as the characteristic that they had engendered in their children, although this is one of the stand-out qualities shown by children who have been nurtured well by their fathers.

Most men do not fully understand just how powerful they can be in the second dimension of fatherlove: nurturing.

One reason is the lack of attention given to the topic by the media, and, in fact, by social scientists, psychologists, and pediatricians. Most past research on child care and development has focused on infant-mother attachment. Among psychologists, the generally accepted theory is that children with a secure attachment to their mothers, especially during infancy, are more likely to feel confident, have good relationships with teachers and peers, and are more likely to be problem solvers. But, until very recently, the father's role as a nurturer has been viewed by many researchers and media as secondary to the mother's.

What's more, in recent decades, men have received a series of conflicting messages and images about just how nurturing fathers are *supposed* to be.

In an early edition of his famous guide to child rearing, *Baby and Child Care,* Dr. Benjamin Spock advised fathers: "A man can be a warm father and a real man at the same time. . . . Of course. I don't mean that the father has to give just as many bottles or change just as many diapers as the mother. But it's fine for him to do these things occasionally. He might make the formula on Sunday." Times change. Today, the revised edition says: "I think that a father with a full-time job—even where a mother is staying home—will do best by his children, by his wife, and himself if he takes on half or more of the management of the children (and also participates in the housework when he gets home from work and on weekends)."

During the 1970s and 1980s, the popular media discovered the "new father" and "Mr. Mom," who were said to be far more nurturing than the "old fathers" of the 1950s. This was the new standard, and it was overblown.

FatherLove

David Blankenhorn, president of the Institute for American Values, points out that the major difference in fathering today, as compared with thirty years ago, is the simple *presence* of the father. Indeed, he suggests that the "old fathers" may not have been so bad after all. He says the media have stereotyped fathers of earlier generations as emotionally distant, absorbed in work, and resistant to the hard work of child care. "It is not surprising that new parents of the baby boom generation—who often act as if what they are doing has never been done in world history—would set up this historical straw father to look good by comparison," he says.

"As a baby boomer myself, I know that my own father does not fit the media stereotype at all. Nor do most of the fathers of the children I grew up with. When it comes to marital commitment and family obligation, many of us new fathers could do worse than to remember our old fathers."[37]

Even if they were emotionally distant, says Blankenhorn, "those fifties dads weren't morally distant. They were home every night." Today's dads, he says, aren't around their kids enough to be a moral presence."[38]

The truth is, we are still finding our way as fathers.

Men cannot breastfeed; we know that. There is something special and feminine about that part of parenting, bottle-feeding notwithstanding. So, if we allow that gender difference to be accepted, then where are the gender-based differences that define fatherhood? Can we define and accept them without being sexist? Is androgynism, at its extreme, analogous to sexism? Like many fathers, I am uncomfortable with these questions. I am uneasy with assuming androgyny, but I am also uncomfortable with traditional gender-based definitions of what makes a good family man; for example, the teaching of physical prowess to my sons. While because of my background I may well be better equipped to teach them about hiking and fishing than my wife, she is the better athlete. Why should either of us be saddled with preconceptions of who is the better teacher in some particular area? She is better at math, and I am better in writing. Is the teaching of one of these subjects by definition more masculine than the other?

A father may or may not nurture his children differently than a mother because of his gender. But the fact that he does nurture, and the reflection of this nurturing in his children, is more important than the culture teaches any of us.

Despite the paucity of studies on fatherhood, considerable evidence does exist of the power of nurturing fatherlove. Every father and potential father should know about this.

• Children with involved fathers are more nurturing and generative, according to the psychiatrist Kyle Pruett. He says these children are much likelier than other kids to raise pets. Says Pruett, "My guess is these kids will find it easier to nurture their own children." This good outcome may be due to something intrinsic about fatherhood as a male occupation, or it may simply be, as Pruett puts it, because two active parents are better than "one and a lump."[39]

• Fathers who spend more time with their young children appear to have an important influence on how compassionate they will be as adults. A twenty-six-year study, the first study of empathy that tracked young children into adulthood, shows that paternal involvement was the single strongest, parent-related factor in adult empathy. The father's influence "was quite astonishing," says the psychologist Richard Koestner of McGill University in Montreal. Fathers who spend time alone with kids more than twice a week—giving baths, meals, and basic care—reared the most compassionate adults.[40] The nurturing of empathy in children, the ability to share another human being's emotions or feelings, is especially important as the bedrock of society, of justice and tolerance in an increasingly fragmented culture. Recent studies have shown that producing empathy in children is not a matter of simply raising "good" or well-behaved children. Quarrelsome, unruly children are as likely to become caring adults as well-behaved children. Nor are empathetic, compassionate adults necessarily the offspring of warm, loving, nurturing parents. Children of nurturing but permissive parents, who fail to set standards of behavior or encourage self-sacrifice, tend to lack compassion as adults.[41]

Among the explanations for the father-empathy link: Dads who spend more time with their kids *model* empathy by being there long enough to care for their kids' needs, or perhaps dads willing to spend a lot of time with their kids are more empathetic themselves. "My hypothesis is that these children do better not because their fathers are more involved, but because their parents as a pair both feel happier with this arrangement," says Michael Lamb, a psychologist with the National Institute of Child Health and Human Development in Bethesda, Maryland. "Father involvement allows both parents to feel that they are achieving and fulfilling themselves." He adds a cautionary note, however, that "there is no benefit to a child in having a father stay home who doesn't want to be there."[42]

• Boys with strong, warm, nurturing fathers are more socially competent, more persistent at solving problems, and more self-directed, according to Norma Radin, a professor at the School of Social Work at the University of Michigan in Ann Arbor, writing in *Social Work in Education*. Among her findings: boys as young as five months who had more contact with their fathers were friendlier with adult strangers than were those who had less. Dallas psychologists John W. Santrock and R. A. Warshak report that boys who lived with their fathers after divorce were warmer, had a higher degree of self-esteem, and were more mature and independent than boys who lived with their mothers. However, when dad isn't present physically or emotionally, boys tend to be more aggressive and less compliant, and they have greater problems in preschool with peer relationships.[43]

Girls with supportive fathers are more likely to be successful in their careers.

"My father loved me unconditionally," says Elisa Sanchez, who directs Trade and Economic Development for Transborder Affairs for San Diego County. She recalls that even when her parents divorced, her father was a strong presence in her life. He continued to support her and her sisters, remembered their birthdays, and made a point of seeing and talking with them as much as possible. Says Veronica Collazo, director of the Office of Training Systems for the U.S. Postal Service, "My father was a tremendous source of encouragement, always so supportive of my activities, whether they were traditional or nontraditional." Both women, who also had strong mothers, credit much of their career success to their father's nurturance.[44]

Journalist Sharon Griffin writes of how her father's strong, nurturing presence shaped her:

In my youth, on hot North Carolina nights, my father would spread a well-worn blanket on a patch of grass in our front yard for me and my brothers to lie on. I would sit beside him, tilt my head back, and gaze at the stars. He didn't tell us stories or anything. He didn't point out constellations, probably because he didn't know any. We just snuggled together, hoping to catch a breeze.

As a Sunday treat, my father liked to take us to watch planes fly off from Smith Reynolds Airport, in Winston-Salem. Not the most fancy or expensive outing, but I never tired of going. He liked to surprise us, too. I remember the time he hid a kitten for me in my mother's closet, even though my mother had threatened to throw me and my father out if he ever brought one home. I am fortunate—privileged—to have memories of my father. More than half of today's black children don't have fathers. . . . For economic reasons alone, a father is vitally needed by black children. But there are other, equally compelling reasons why these children are in need of a father. No one is born with a strong sense of self esteem—with pride; we learn these qualities from our mothers and fathers: our first and most influential role models. Positive role models for a child are as essential as food on the table. . . .

My father taught me so much, and mostly by his example. My father never made an issue of being black. He is black, positive, and proud. So am I. By the time a white person first called me "nigger," when I was in college, I was already too proud and self-assured to let the word and its implications get me down. . . . I am somebody because my father helped me to be somebody. I don't let the stigma of being black in this country overwhelm me, thanks to the example my father set for me. He believed in me, and through him I learned to believe in myself.[45]

Fathers are also the primary influence regarding sex roles for sons and daughters. A father who is powerful, nurturing, and available is usually seen as a role model by a son; a weak father is less likely to be imitated. A growing body of research shows that boys as young as three years old are searching for masculine models on which to build their sense of self, but as Samuel Osherson, author of *Finding Our Fathers* writes, "the urge to identify with father creates the crucial dilemma for boys. Boys have to give up mother for father, but who is father?"[46]

Men growing up without a good gender model grow up with an inflated, hypermasculine view of manhood, and are therefore more prone to violence. Paul Lewis, president of an impressive parenting education program in San Diego called Family University (which offers a course in fathering called Dads University), along with Ken Canfield's National Center for Fathering, investigated the images of fatherhood held by one hundred Minnesota prison inmates. They were asked to describe men whom they considered father figures. Less than 12 percent even put their own fathers on the list; 52 percent named sports or entertainment heroes as their father figures. "I work with a number of people who work with juvenile delinquent kids. I've never had a single case worker who has ever had a kid report a healthy relationship with their dad. Not one out of hundreds," says Lewis.

Lewis and other academic researchers are also convinced that the father's role is as important, and possibly more important, than the mother's in giving the son or the daughter confidence in sexual identity. "I'm convinced by the available research, and after working with thousands of families, that when fathers withdraw from their adolescent daughters because of discomfort with their daughter's sexuality, that this sets the stage for the daughter's sexual experimentation or promiscuity; the daughters are looking for the closeness that has been withdrawn by their fathers." A daughter looks to her father to confirm her attractiveness; when that is withheld, she looks elsewhere—often with a sense of desperation.

A similar process is true for how boys view their sexuality. The father who is affectionate to his son, rather than standoffish, is able to give a son a view of manhood that is more whole; as the son grows up, he is likely to be more confident in his expression of manliness.

What about the father, how is he affected by his own nurturing fatherlove; how is his life enriched? We know that fathers who do not have the experience of nurturing their children often feel longing, anger, and grief. "The grief work that I see takes the form of feeling guilty, feeling as if everything bad that happens is my fault," says pediatrician T. Berry Brazelton, MD. "Even twelve years later, if something goes wrong, it's my fault because I wasn't there those first few months."[47]

There has been a great silence among fathers, about fathering—most specifically, a silence about what fathering does for a man: the payoff for *him*. And the emotional costs of not doing it.

During a trip to New York, I visited with an old friend. Actually, I had not known him that well. In high school he had been smart and witty, one of those guys who thought he was too good for Kansas, who walked down the hall and looked right over you or through you, as if you didn't exist. Or at least that's the way he remembers himself.

"The truth was, I was busy disappearing," he said. We were sitting in his office high above Manhattan. Today, he is a successful corporate lawyer.

"I've been disappearing all my life," he said. "Professionally, this works well for me. It's a way of not being in the room, of disconnecting from people. I can look them in the eye, nod appropriately and make noises, and yet I'm not really listening. I'm on to the next case."

But disappearing does not work well in a family.

"One day during a ride up to the farm with my wife sitting next to me, I realized I was holding an imaginary conversation with her. She was sitting right there. Why wasn't I talking to *her?*"

Everybody does that, I said, some of the time.

"Sure they do," he said. "And anybody watching a couple doing that at, say a restaurant, would think: There's an old married couple not talking to each other. But they're not dead; something is going on in their heads. They're probably having an imaginary conversation with somebody, maybe with each other."

As he discovered, disappearing from a child can be more difficult.

His first child, *in utero,* had a syndrome that causes severe deformities in the skull and spine, and the absence of kidneys. In a second trimester abortion, which the doctors advised, labor was induced, and the baby was born dead.

My friend did not disappear then. He was with his wife throughout the hideous night, as a blizzard howled outside the hospital window. "You understand, I don't disappear during a crisis. That's one of the ways I have masked my everyday absences. And it's not that I don't spend time with my family. I do. That's why I'm a company lawyer instead of a member of a firm. The hours are predictable. I can be with my family."

But being with his family emotionally was different from being with them physically. He began to see that shortly after the birth of his daughter, Judith.

FatherLove

During her first year, he became increasingly anxious, and he did not know why. He ascribed his nervousness to ordinary causes: job; physical health; turning forty. But slowly he realized that this tension was associated with his daughter.

"I was withdrawing from her. This withdrawing was happening every day. She would come toddling into the room, and I would start listening to the radio, or I would start to walk into another room, and my tension would build. I could feel it physically. It was a tingling sensation."

He was disappearing in front of his daughter, just as he remembered his mother had done when he was a child.

He could not con or charm his daughter, he could not make a case, file a brief, slap her on the back to make it all right. He could see this in her eyes; he could see that she knew. And he knew that if he continued, then someday she would disappear, and he would lose her.

He decided to do something about his disappearing act.

The astonishing thing, he says, is that it took so long for a highly educated professional to figure out how to reappear. But this was a lifelong pattern, more ingrained than the usual parental distraction. The changes were simple but very difficult.

"When I found myself walking past my daughter as she approached me, I would say to myself, sometimes out loud, *'Stop.* Turn around. Go back back in there and play with your daughter.' "

Feeling overwrought, he would walk back to her, get down on his hands and knees, and play with her. He would look her in the eye and talk to her. He would focus on her as a person—as a *person,* not as a child. And his feelings of tension and unease would fade, at least temporarily.

He practiced over and over. Sometimes he forgot; sometimes he began to slip away again and then would snap himself back into focus. He began to see his own reflection return to his daughter's eyes.

"I had always been a nervous person. I had come to think of my never-ending tension as chronic background noise. I had assumed that this was just the way life was and always would be, at least for me. Well, it's astonishing how much of that can go away.

"First it went away when I was with my daughter, and then I began to focus on my wife. *'Look at her, talk to her'* "

He even began to do this with people he worked with, and it transformed his relationships with them. "Simple things, nothing profound."

But if not for his daughter, he said, he might have vanished completely.

For three decades American fathers have moved along two separate paths—the nurturant father and the absent father. University of Pennsylvania sociologist Frank F. Furstenberg, Jr., says the "two faces of fatherhood" sometimes coexist in the same man—men who come and go, who do not have or share custody, who seem caught in a paternal purgatory.[48] During the past thirty years, the divorce rate has tripled, and the rate of out-of-wedlock births had quadrupled. Consequently, men between the ages of twenty and forty-nine spend an average of only seven years living in a house with young children, a decline of nearly 50 percent in three decades.[49]

At the same time, many fathers have become involved in their children's lives in areas in which their own fathers were excluded.

For example, fathers are now likely to be present in the

delivery room, an experience that our fathers never had. This experience, increasing in frequency, often has a profound influence on a father and his children. One study found that of twenty deeply involved dads, all but one witnessed their children's births.[50] This is one of the most positive changes about fathering today.

In my own life, few events compare with the births of my two sons: holding Jason to the light to see his first day, calming Matthew by placing my hand on his chest and tummy, seconds after a traumatic birth, and being there with my wife, breathing with her, connecting with her in that oddly sexual way. The only comparable experience was holding my mother as she died, squeezing her hand, trying to breathe her life back, and feeling both enraged and empty by what I felt was my failure. That was the reversed mirror image of the birth of my sons.

By some accounts, more than 40 percent of America's dads are intimately involved with everything from childbirth to diaper changing to running the kids to play dates in the family station wagon. The dads aren't only highly educated liberal intellectuals determined to be more sensitive than their own fathers, but also conservative, churchgoing, blue-collar men who have discovered how much fathering enriches their lives.[51]

In general, today's fathers are doing better in two areas, according to a long-term study of American family life by Massachusetts Mutual Life Insurance. Americans think today's fathers do better at spending playtime with children and helping children in school; these are the same two areas in which yesterday's fathers ranked lowest. At the same time, more than half think today's fathers do less well at discipline, something three-fourths say their own fathers were at least as good at.

When asked in this study what the biggest change will

be for fathers in the next ten years, the most common response was that fathers will spend more time with their families. But wishing will not make it so.

In general, parents spend about 40 percent less time with their children than parents did in 1965. Lettie Pogrebin, in *Family Politics* and *Growing Up Free*, advocates "more dad and less mom" in the family. According to Pogrebin's disturbing study of how much time men spend with their children, the average father interacts with his baby less than thirty-eight seconds a day. Dads don't make much of an impression in thirty-eight seconds: half of the three-to-four year olds in the study preferred watching TV to spending time with their fathers. The good news: the other half still wished their fathers would spend more time with them. "When playtime is measured," Pogrebin comments, "fathers may well equal or even surpass mothers." By contrast, when *caregiving* time is measured, fathers are largely absent.[52]

This pattern starts early. Psychologists Sharron Humenick and Larry Bugen were dismayed to find that most studies portray early parenting largely in terms of mothering. They interviewed thirty-seven middle-class couples attending Lamaze classes in a university community. They then compared how much time each parent spent actively involved with the baby with how much time the parent had predicted to spend before the baby was born. The mothers ended up spending *more* time holding, feeding, changing, and touching than they had anticipated. The fathers spent *less* time than expected on every item—changing, touching, washing, playing, or talking. Only three of the fathers spent more time with their babies than had been predicted. Because the child, during the first few weeks of its life, initiates about half of the parent-child interactions, dads can lag far behind moms in picking up the infant's cues; both dad and mom are frustrated—mom is frustrated because she's doing more than she anticipated; dad is frustrated because he's not bonding with the baby as much as he had desired.[53]

Those men who do manage to be with their babies and children have been dubbed Mr. Moms, a title that robs them of their identity as fathers and intimates they are substitutes for the "real" parent. During the past decade, the popular press has paid considerable attention to Mr. Mom. But contrary to the coverage, house husbands are still rare, and therefore isolated and misunderstood.

"It's still difficult for the man and for society," says Dr. Kyle Pruett, a clinical professor of psychiatry at the Yale School of Medicine's Child Study Center, who has done a five-year study of stay-at-home fathers. "Most men find themselves explaining what they're doing with the child at the supermarket week after week. The first response they get is, 'Isn't that lovely—you're baby-sitting!' But when it keeps happening, most men get pretty perturbed."[54]

One former house husband, a commercial artist who stayed home with his daughter for five years while he free-lanced and his wife worked as an accountant, tells me he loved every minute of the experience—except that his wife viewed him as less than a man because he *did* enjoy staying home with his daughter. He now blames his divorce, in part, on being a house husband, but he would not trade the experience, even for a healed marriage.

Another at-home dad, Ted Bzdega, thirty-eight, of Des Moines, described the fullness of his life:

My wife is a physician and makes a good living work-ing many hours. I'm a product of the late sixties and early seventies. I'm fluid and open to a lot of ideas. I don't find the pressure in being a house dad as much as some of my friends would. It would drive them nuts. We live out on a seventy-acre farm, so I don't have a life much beyond the kids. I'm always there. The tough thing is your day doesn't have as much structure to it. But I sort of feel guilty that I'm having so much fun with my kids when my wife is going out to work. She feels guilty about not being here as much. My kids think that I'm a friend, but not necessarily a friend they would pick out at school. They look at me as a big grown-up kid, and sometimes I feel that I'm becoming a kid again. I'm getting a second childhood.

When forced to loosen their grip on breadwinning as their primary identity, some men discover other dimensions of their fatherhood and their manhood.

Cory Sorenson, of Rifle, Colorado, who had spoken so eloquently of his pride in hanging drywall and his work connection to his father, also described how his mother had taught him the other skills that he would later need. Cory is out of work because of a serious back injury. He stays home with his children in their trailer, isolated, without a phone, but enjoying this new role. His wife is the breadwinner now, and perhaps for the next few years because of his injury. He says it's hard for him to explain how much he loves being the nurturer.

I love my kids, and I want to take care of them the best way I know how. In order to do that, I've got to be that kind of a person, gentle. When I was growing up, I was a pretty hard-core person myself. I was kind of the bully of the crowd I ran around with. I'd go to Aspen just to pick a fight, just to have something to do. Now I have kids, and I'm going to do the best job I can to make sure that they get raised right.

It's been real hard on me, being laid up, and real hard on my wife. I'm used to getting up at six in the morning, going to work all day, working till five or six at night and coming home. Now she gets up and goes to work, and I stay at home with the kids. It's a big difference. I've learned that there's a lot more to home life, to raising the kids, than I really realized. Before, I thought, "You had a pretty easy day, you just stayed home and took care of the kids." Now I realize that it's like a forty-eight-hour-a-day job watching the kids. When I was hanging Sheetrock for a living, that's hard work, but when I got home, I still had energy because I had the fluids going from hanging Sheetrock all day. It was tiring, but now I get just as tired staying home chasing after the kids, changing the diapers, the whole nine yards. It's hard to say whether this is as hard as hanging Sheetrock because now I've got an injury to slow me down, but maybe it is. In a way, hanging Sheetrock was easier on me because I could take my frustrations out on the work. I would never hit my kids, it's one of my strong beliefs.

I just love my kids, I love being around them and before, when I was working, I only saw them at night. There's a closer bond now than there was before. When my boy was real little, he always went to Janet. He was kind of a momma's boy. And now, when he gets hurt or something, he comes running to dad. He's becoming a daddy's boy. It's a neat feeling; I don't know how to describe it.

Pruett's study of stay-at-home fathers and their children has shown that dads developed an "anti-Rambo" attitude.

"They were less defensively macho. Caring for another human being changes us all, men and women. It humanizes us. . . . The fathers become more considerate of their friends and families, find themselves more interested in human relationships, and are less competitive. But they don't lose their business sense or their edge. One father who kept at his real estate business said he became more efficient at negotiation because he learned to read people better."[55]

Another expanding group of dads, single fathers, are not quite so positive about their experiences. I asked one single father what it's like.

"Mainly, you feel isolated," he said. "Like when you pick up your kid at school. All the mothers are there talking among themselves, and they look at you like you're something special—a freak, really. That kind of special."

Special indeed. Single dads, still greatly outnumbered by single moms, are going to get a lot more attention in the future, if not more respect. More than 1.8 million dads are doing the job alone, according to U.S. Census figures. Between 1985 and 1989, their number grew three times faster than single moms. And one subgroup, families headed by fathers who have never married, has grown the fastest of any group.

Much of the phenomenon is due to the revolution in divorce laws during the 1980s, particularly in California. Judges today are more willing to award custody or joint custody to fathers, although this shift toward paternal custody has met with stinging criticism from some psychologists and others who view it as court-sanctioned retrosexism.

The jury is still out on whether or not the trend is good for children. Some studies conclude that boys do better than girls with dads, but girls raised by dads can thrive, too. And women can do just fine raising boys on their own, especially if they cultivate male role models for their sons. But the more the experts study single parenting, the clearer it becomes that the quality of the individual parent matters more than the gender. Even so, the single father is often caught in a bind: praised for being special but suspected for being different.

"Women communicate among themselves better than men," said a single dad whose own father died when he was four. "I can't turn to other single dads because they're too harried, but of course, so are single moms. Married men usually show up at school functions because their wives want them to; they participate to the degree that their wives insist they do.

"I can't call mothers for advice, either. I might be considered a single male on the hunt, true or not. You can't socialize with married ladies."

I asked a single mom, a friend, what she thought of this man's sense of isolation. She has joint custody of two daughters with her ex-husband. She pointed out the income gap that exists between single moms and single dads. (Single mothers earn an average of $13,100 annually; single fathers earn an average of $29,000, but they do lag behind married-couple families, and one in six is poor.)

"He also doesn't mention that single fathers get preferential treatment," she said. "I see this special treatment in the way teachers deal with my ex-husband. One time there was a potluck dinner at my older daughter's school, and every parent was expected to bring a dish. The school let him slide on this, probably because he was a man. My daughter felt terrible; she felt different, excluded. I work longer hours than my ex-husband, and it's harder for me to pick up my daughter on time, every time. They're more accommodating to my ex-husband, helping him make special arrangements for pickup when he's going to be out of town or at a social engagement."

Perhaps single fatherhood is a new battleground in the war of the sexes. Or maybe the growing number of single dads and moms could become allies in the workplace. The single dad who spoke with me believes his experience has made him more understanding toward single moms.

"I have no doubt their burden is great," he said. "First, their earning power is less. Second, I can't imagine how hard it must be for single moms to raise teenage boys. These guys are tough. They're physically very strong, they tell you to go to hell, they need tremendous discipline.

"Whether you're a single dad or a single mom, you give up most of your social life," he continued. "You give up status in the community. Working married dads have status, they do lunch. But this is my choice. I choose not to attend after-hours business meetings.

"When I was married and worked full-time outside the house, I defined myself by my job. That was my manhood. Now I look at my boys and realize that I am helping them turn into men. I see them changing from soft, pudgy children with all the emotions of children; I see them becoming the kind of people whose word you can rely on. That's my image of a man. And I want to be a man who is there for them."

Why aren't more fathers nurturing to their children— and their wives? In part, the reason is related to the lack of value placed by the culture on nurturing fathers. But that is changing. One mother said:

When I think of my own father, I think of fatherhood as being a chore. Simply because he wasn't particularly nurturing. I don't think fathers saw their role as being nurturing in the 1950s and '60s. I think it's different now; sometimes I see my husband coming home from work, and I see him perceiving fatherhood as a chore, but he fights that perception. Whereas when I was a child, men didn't fight it. It was a chore. If you were a man, you worked hard, you were the breadwinner, and that's what you did. Mainly you played with your kids on the weekend, but it wasn't your job to be a nurturer during the week. You did your job, you came home, you had dinner because it was on the table, you watched TV. Whatever juice you gave your kids was a plus, but it certainly wasn't a requirement, not in my house.

For some fathers with sons, fear of nurturing can be linked to homophobia. But more widespread reasons are anxiety over money and fear of disappointment: the suspicion that our children will be disappointed with us as breadwinners or that our nurturing will somehow be rejected, particularly during adolescence.

One problem that most couples must overcome if the father is to be more involved with his family is the hidden power dispute over nurturing.

"The mother is the gatekeeper to fatherhood," says Dr. Michael J. Diamond, associate clinical professor of psychiatry at UCLA. "She may allow it or obstruct."[56]

Some women do obstruct it, for a subtle and understandable reason: Few people give up power in one area without a struggle when they may lack power in other areas—the workplace, for example, which is still dominated by males.

"For many women, it's apparently better to maintain responsibility for parenthood, even at the cost of what we might call role overload, rather than yield some of that status and responsibility to a partner," says Michael Lamb, a psychologist with the National Institute of Child Health and Human Development.[57]

This sense of competitiveness seems to increase the more educated a woman is. A Boston University study showed that the older a mother was, and the higher her educational level and previous job status, the more she monopolized parenting. "If women were as truthful as possible, they'd admit it's difficult both to ask husbands for help and to give over some of the responsibility," says Judith Auerbach, a sociologist and former director of the Institute for the Study of Women and Men at the University of Southern California. "Women feel that they're supposed to want to be involved, and if they're not, then there's something wrong with them."[58]

Indiana University sociologist Linda Haas suggests that the working women who most welcome dad's help share three traits: They don't feel guilty about their jobs; their own fathers helped raise them; and their husbands have flexible hours. One mother told me:

Something happened when our first daughter was six months old. We were suffering through colic. I was crying, she was crying, and my husband took her from me. I said, "No, *I* need to take care of her; I need to do this." And he looked at me, and he was really startled, and he said, *"She's my daughter too,* and just because it's your way doesn't mean it's the right way." I just assumed that I was the mom, I was the nurturer, I was doing it the right way. And damned if that child didn't stop crying anyway, just to spite me. (She laughs.) It really was a wake-up call to me, that he has instincts toward his children and he acts on them, and it's not like when my father used to come in the door and my mother would say, "You kids go back in your room and I'll call you when dinner's ready." She protected our father from us.

Kyle Pruett advises mothers to expect such territorial feelings and not to squash them. "Talk about it. Humor is the best way to cope." He suggests that fathers not rise to the competition. "If you learn some secret about your baby, don't keep it from the mother."[59] And Dr. Ronald Levant, a Harvard Medical School psychologist who calls the home "the next frontier for men," suggests that dad can be more of a partner in the home and less of an employee to the wife if the dad assumes total responsibility for a certain aspect of housework or child care; for example, he might get the kids ready for school, and she might get them ready for bed.

One cautionary note for the nurturing fatherman: Fathers who try hard to connect with their children, to be superdads, sometimes lose touch with their wives. Levine advises the men enrolled in his fathering sessions to schedule dates with their wives. He says, "Dating your wife has a dramatic effect on being able to connect with your kids. After all, you are a family."[60]

Michael Lamb advises that increased involvement by fathers is most effective when it makes mothers' lives happier.

A second problem is, where does parenthood leave off and fatherhood begin?

Dr. Michael J. Diamond, the UCLA professor, says that fathers shouldn't turn themselves into "junior mothers" and that children do not need two competing moms, but parents who help each other. "The father's role is to serve as a structuring presence. He should be challenging. Pushing his child ahead. Leading the child to the outer world.

Mentoring. One way the father introduces the child to the world is through play." Indeed, some pioneering research at the University of California at Davis found that, in addition to being good baby-sitters, adult male rhesus monkeys play more with baby monkeys than do mother monkeys. Monkey dads and human dads, says Diamond, evoke play. "And play is a way to achieve mastery. It encourages mastery in the sense of being able to deal with phenomena. They don't control you; you control them. You're the rider on the horse; you aren't simply dragged along by it. The father gives you the sense of riding the horse. Of riding life."[61]

What do children have to say about changing gender roles at home? Children's Express is a nonprofit news service where children are the reporters. Tape-recorded interviews and comments are edited by teenagers and adults, then published. Here is how some kids view the housework roles of their fathers and mothers:

> Suki Cheong, thirteen: Even if the woman is working, it hasn't changed in terms of how much housework she does and how much she takes care of the kids and stuff like that. Lots of times, even if the guy knows the woman is working, he doesn't do anything anyway.
> Bip Selkirk, thirteen: My mother will say, "Okay, everybody, now we have to help clean the house." My father will go to his little closet and start putting screws away or fixing his hammer. He doesn't help much around the house; he fixes his own stuff most of the time.
> Yemi Falade, thirteen: My mother can't cook at all,

and she hates cooking, so she's always sending out for food, and my father's always complaining. He says, "You're my wife. You're supposed to have fixed my food."

Suki: You just don't see your dad doing things like cooking or doing laundry. It's sort of entrenched that your mother should do these things. It's kind of hard to imagine your dad doing them, even if your mom works.

Stephanie Kolin, twelve: I think we should try [to keep up feminism] because men are trying to forget. No offense, but they are. So we have to keep trying to get farther and farther. Not ahead of men, but keep trying to get as many equal rights as they have.[62]

Most days, I agree with columnist Dave Barry, who writes: "The major issue facing a man and a woman who decide to live together is: Dirt. I am serious. Men and women don't even *see* dirt the same way. Women, for some hormonal reason, can see individual dirt molecules, whereas men tend not to notice them until they join together into clumps large enough to support commercial agriculture."[63] But on other days, the better angels of my nature remind me that when I do housework, I am nurturing my wife and children. This is not a concept that comes easily or naturally.

In fact, upon looking into the evolution of housework, one finds that this is a recent and somewhat unnatural role for men *and* women. As Debbie Taylor writes in *New Internationalist*, "Women in the industrialized world did not gather together over tea one afternoon and agree to work unpaid at cleaning, cooking, laundry, child care, and nursing out of the sheer kindness of their hearts. No, they were given little choice. They were, as Ivan Illich put it, 'flattered and threatened, by capitalist and cleric' into the current situation." Sociologist Anne Oakley writes: "Other cultures may live in families, but they do not necessarily have housewives. They have women, men, and children whose labor is woven together to create a home and livelihood for the whole family." As Taylor points out, in Kenya housework is interwoven with agriculture:

> As a woman in Kenya, for instance, starts to untie the shawl securing a baby to her back so she can wield her hoe with more freedom among the maize stalks, another child will be there to take the baby from her. While she works, her daughters will be pounding sorghum and fetching water for the evening meal, her sons driving goats and cattle to fresh grazing, her husband sinking wooden poles into the ground for a new house.
>
> All of these activities are work, but those that we would term housework are so intricately interwoven with agriculture that it is difficult to tease them apart. The growing of food and the growing of children are both vital to the family's survival. Without children the food cannot be grown; without food there can be no children. Who would dare make the judgment that holding your youngest baby on your lap is less important than weeding a few more yards in the maize field.[64]

The Industrial Revolution delegated work in the home to women and narrowed the father's role to that of breadwinner.

Taylor points out that in the early days of the Industrial Revolution, in the 1840s and 1850s, "factory and mine owners did not care who did their work for them and hired whole families to dig coal or weave cloth in the textile mills." This pattern might have continued except for the dreadfully high infant mortality rate in the city slums and the introduction of more efficient machines that reduced the need for so many workers. The housewife was born: segregated from the economy outside the home, just as men were segregated from the life of home and much of the intimacy of child rearing. "In 1737, more than 98 percent of married women in England worked outside the home," writes Taylor. "By 1911, more than 90 percent were employed solely as housewives. And this pattern was repeated throughout the industrialized world."[65] Taylor goes on to express an interesting point of view about where fathers fit into the current debate over housework:

> There is a part (a very small part) of me that sympathizes with them. Men perceive that equating love and domestic work is a trap. They fear that to get involved with housework would send them hurtling into the bottomless pit of self-sacrifice that is women's current caring role. As soon as they do attempt a smidgin of housework, they often find themselves caught up in a wrangle with women about "standards" of cleanliness—a wrangle that is really about deciding when enough is enough.

Arlie Hochschild, author of *The Second Shift*, states that the questions of who does what and what needs doing can become the sources of deep tension in a marriage. In the families that Hochschild studied over an eight-year period, the fact that wives worked outside the home did not account for why some marriages were happy and others were not; what contributed to happiness was the husband's willingness to share the work at home. Whether traditional or more egalitarian, couples were happier when the men did a sizable share of housework and child care. She points out that in one study of six hundred couples filing for divorce, the second most common reason women cited for wanting to divorce, after "mental cruelty," was their husbands' neglect of home or children. Women mentioned this reason more than finances, physical abuse, drinking, or infidelity. Hochschild's study found that, when hours of work outside and inside the home were added up, women in the 1960s and 1970s worked roughly fifteen more hours each week than men. Over a year, they worked an extra month of twenty-four-hour days. Over a dozen years, they worked an extra year of twenty-four-hour days.

Most women, according to Hochschild, work one shift at the office or factory and a "second shift" at home. She came to believe that "those husbands who helped very little at home were often just as deeply affected as their wives—through the resentment their wives felt toward them and through their own need to steel themselves against that resentment. . . . Even when husbands happily shared the work, their wives felt more responsible for home and children. More women than men kept track of doctor's appointments and arranged for kids' playmates to come over." Also, she found, when men did participate in the care of their children, they chose more of the fun jobs, for example, taking their kids to the park while the wife did the dishes.[66]

The home front may be improving. *American Demographics* magazine reports that research done from the mid-1960s to the mid-1980s shows that gradually men have been doing a greater share of housework since 1965. Men have gone from five to twenty hours of housework a week (in 1985). That would seem to be an impressive increase, except that men still only do one fifth of the cooking, cleaning, and laundry.[67]

"We're in the midst of an evolution," says James Levine

of The Fatherhood Project, in *American Health,* "not a revolution." One study of egalitarian marriages showed that the most involved dads did about 57 percent of the parental work, but the most involved mothers do 78 percent; the average father spends about 5.5 hours a week alone with his children (not necessarily interacting) to his wife's 19.5.

Alix Finklestein, senior editor of *Parents* magazine, reports that in focus groups run by her publication, "the younger couples just don't experience as much friction over housework and child care. We see a good trend happening."

But is this progress occurring fast enough? Are sons and daughters being raised today to view the dad as a partner in housework and child care?

One recent study suggests that some pessimism is natural: It shows that teenage sons in two-earner households goof off while daughters do more work; the sons spend less time on chores in dual-career marriages than the sons in families where the wife stays at home. Sons in two-career marriages spend less than three hours a week on household chores, while teenage daughters in two-career families spend ten hours a week on cooking, laundry, and car and household repairs. According to Mary Holland Benin, an associate professor at Arizona State University and co-author of the study, parents may see daughters as more willing and trustworthy to do the chores. "Mothers may think, 'Oh, my son will ruin my good blouse. He'll wash it in hot water.' "[68]

If you want to stop men from vanishing as fathers, start with the dishes when they're boys. That was the message I heard from a group of mothers sitting around a table at Muir Elementary School in Seattle, Washington.

Gloria Nichols, a mother in her thirties who has fought hard to get off welfare and now works part-time for the school district, described the domestic double standard and poverty that she experienced as a girl.

"My dad worked and scraped to make a living for us and bring home food. I had eight brothers and two sisters. I had to wash out diapers, I had to use the scrub board. My brothers, they'd go outside and kick it. They'd do nothing.

"I ate out of garbage cans. I contemplated suicide at age twelve because I figured if my butt was not around, there would be more food for my brothers. I'm not ashamed to say I stole. My brothers stole. The difference was I stole for my family, my brothers stole for themselves."

When she was thirteen, instead of killing herself, she lied about her age and got a good baby-sitting job, to help support her family.

Most of the mothers sitting around the table are single parents and African-American. But they were quick to point out that the double standard in the life of children is not limited to any particular racial or ethnic group. And don't get them wrong, they said, they're not knocking men.

Leona Westmoreland spoke admiringly of her husband. "I've been fortunate enough to be married to a strong, confident black man for twenty-two years," she said. "He picks up the kids at school. He cleans, he cooks, and he still works eighteen hours a day. His parents taught him to be a man and a mother at the same time, to care about a male child and a female child the same."

And Phyllis Yasutake, an actress and the mother of four boys and two girls at the school, spoke movingly of her father, married to her mother for forty-eight years. "My father sewed the buttons on my skirt," she said. "My father clipped my nails. My father sat in on my band concerts at Franklin High and fell asleep in the front row. And he snored loud, and I'd say, 'That's good, he's here.' "

Yasutake and Westmoreland credited much of their personal strength to the fact that their fathers were involved in daily domestic life. But most of the women described a different experience.

One women said matter-of-factly, "Me and my sister had to make up our brothers' beds, clean their rooms. They had no responsibility. I rarely played outside. At the age of seven or eight, I was cooking and doing all the housework. I can see the same thing happening now in my family. My two younger boys aren't handling their responsibilities, but the girl is. I want to teach them differently, but I guess I fall back."

Eventually, the domestic double standard can become a sexual double standard.

"You don't teach equal responsibility early, look what happens," said June Sanders, a bookkeeper and parent.

"Magic Johnson, everybody feels bad about what happened to him, but does anybody feel bad about the hundreds of women he may have given that virus to? If a woman stood up on TV and said, 'I've got AIDS, I've had sex with hundreds of men,' she'd be called . . ."

"A tramp," someone said.

"That's right. No one feels the pain of those women. That's the way our society is," Sanders said. "That's the double standard that begins when men are boys and women are girls." One that for many children begins with housework.

Nichols, the woman who had considered suicide as a girl, said the first step is to educate parents about the need to end this domestic double standard. The road to self-sufficiency and responsibility, she said, begins at home. "When I get my sons up in the morning, I tell them to wash the dishes, run the vacuum, and I tell them over and over that there's a reason for them to do this. They don't understand the reason now, but maybe someday they will."

Many fathers are hungry to learn more about their nurturing dimension. A number of programs have sprung up around the country to fulfill that need.

Paul Lewis started Family University in San Diego several years ago; part of his curriculum is called the College of Fathering, or Dads University. He started the program, and accompanying newsletter, after having lunch with a friend and discussing the divorce of a couple no one had suspected would split up.

"We began to wonder why we wouldn't be next," he says. "We didn't want to be next. Then we got to thinking about why we didn't do more planning to be fathers." In 1978, they launched a newsletter called "Dads Only." "The focus of it has been to put in the hands of busy guys ways to interact with their kids, how to keep their marriage fresh. The idea is to be preventive rather than remedial. My conviction is that a lot of men care deeply about their families, but their careers are on the fast track, and small parenting problems become big ones before they know it."

Dads U followed with a short curriculum, hosted around the country by community groups, churches, and companies that care about helping men and fathers. The curriculum, which has been taught to nearly three thousand fathers, includes programs called "Secrets of Fast Track Fathering." Others: "Fathering Competence: Shaping Your Winning Style"; and the "Seven Secrets of Successful Kids."

"Often, this course is a bridge for men to talk about restoring a healthy relationship with their own fathers. We regularly have guys in our course who are divorced; even if they're noncustodial dads, they want to do what is right for their kids." His approach focuses on nurturing, not breadwinning. "I've pondered many times: What in our culture is there that gives fathers permission to abandon a child without feeling bad about it? Mothers do not feel okay about it, but fathers do it in droves."

The cultural message is clear: A father can abandon his kids emotionally as long as he is a provider. As a culture, we've lost touch with the fact that the father's participation and contribution to the daily life of the family, in the home, is essential. Fathers bring home the bacon. But now we know that mothers can provide just as well, and suddenly we don't feel so important. We've tried working harder, and that doesn't fulfill us; if we exist, as fathers, *only* within that first dimension, as breadwinners, we eventually disappear.

Lewis is profiting from the hunger in fathers to learn more about nurturing. He would like to see more work-places offer on-site courses in fathering and mothering. But Lewis has come to believe that we cannot wait until men realize their hunger to be multidimensional dads.

"Family skills in America are in pieces," he says, "We're seeing more and more people starting families who don't have a clue. Are we going to put our finger in the dike, or are we going to rebuild it?"

I asked a group of teenagers at San Diego's Garfield High School, a special facility for teenagers who have not suc-ceeded in traditional schools, what they knew and what they did not know about parenting. Like the teenagers I interviewed in Wisconsin, these young people hadn't a clue. The difference between these young people and the ones I interviewed in Wisconsin, however, is that most of these teenagers are already parents.

"I want to be that Cliff Huxtable family," said one boy. "I want that perfect kind of family."

I asked: Has anyone ever talked to you about how to become a father like Cliff Huxtable (aka Bill Cosby)?

He shook his head and looked at me like I was crazy.

For some of these boys, becoming a good father is about as mysterious a process as getting an MBA from Harvard.

"It's fear and amazement you feel," says one teenage boy, describing how it felt when he became a dad. "Because all you hear about is you're not supposed to have kids until you get your shit together—excuse my language—until you have a house, car, a dog . . . and then you have kids. My dad, he don't help me know how to be one. He starts ragging on me because I don't want to go to L.A. with him because I got a job interview in San Diego. He tries to grab at my throat, and my brother comes and snaps him on the couch. My dad says to my brother, 'Do you want me to put a bullet in your head?' "

Another boy, who is sixteen, explains what he knows about fatherhood. "A single mother, she always teaches her first child to watch out for the next one. Then she teaches the next one to watch out for the next one, all the way down the line. If my brother died right now, I would be my niece's father."

Where do they turn? Not that many years ago, if a child had a bad father, or no father, he or she could at least absorb some sense of fathering from men in the neighborhood. But today the number of fatherless children is fast reaching a level comparable to the number of fathered children.

So who teaches these kids how to be parents? Television? Has anyone told them that good fathering is more than the absence of violence, more than bringing home the bacon, more even than the list of chores on the refrigerator door? Unless future or current fathers *know* their power, they will be unlikely to value it as much as they should or nurture it in themselves.

Ironically, young mothers at Garfield are required to attend classes in parenting and infant development, while young fathers are not. The boys in the classroom today have been invited for the discussion.

I ask the girls: Does a child need a father?

"Yeah, for a boy, you need a father for potty training," says one of the young single moms. Based on her experience, she's fatalistic. "The only way you're going to get them to take care of their baby is drop it off and don't come back." One fourteen-year-old says she's not going to marry her baby's father, or maybe any man, because she believes that males impregnate girls "to tie the women down, so you can't go anywhere, but they can go party and do what they want."

Judy Kirsten, a teacher who has worked with Garfield's pregnant minors' program for years, says the kids in this class aren't much different from most teenagers. "When it comes to parenting knowledge—especially knowledge about fatherhood—teenagers in any school live in a fantasyland," she says.

One boy explains patiently what he thinks is the first rule of marriage, which he says he has learned from media and from experience: "You have to have like fifty-fifty, love and hate. No fighting, no love. Usually the love fades away." Several of them say their fathers have never said "I love you" to them. A boy explains, "Fathers have a different way."

In their experience, what percentage of media messages about fatherhood have been positive?

"I'd say about two percent," says one girl. What about motherhood? "That's about ten percent."

I wonder: Do these kids know that child abuse is often born from parental ignorance? With no knowledge of child development, a young parent may not know that a two-year-old is incapable of bladder control, and so when the child wets the bed, the parent picks him up and begins to shake him.

If your parents aren't around, I ask them, who should teach you about parenting? School? Churches? Television?

"Everybody watches TV," says one girl. "Mostly when you watch TV, it's about dads molesting little girls. They should show the dad taking part with the baby, and more with the mom."

"Education," says one of the boys. "Educate us men while we're still young, through school, through church, somewhere."

The fourteen-year-old mom wonders; "Why isn't this kind of class required for all kids, before they become parents?"

Good question.

Here's a proposal, one way to rebuild the dike. Starting next year, every high school student in America should, in order to graduate, be required to take a course in parenting and child development. Worried about public schools dictating family values? Don't be. This is one area where a voucher program (possibly with no exchange of money) could work.

Here's what the school should say to students and their parents:

You're required to take (5, 10, 50?) hours of instruction in parenting. Go out into the community and find a course. Go to your church, your synagogue, your Buddhist temple. Go to the YMCA. Go to Planned Parenthood. Go to a course offered by some public-service-oriented corporation. Within reason, we don't care where you go to discuss family issues; we just require you to go do it. If you can't find a course out there, this school will offer you one as a last resort.

Why do we need such an approach? Because the success of our schools is determined more by the emotional and physical health of children than by any kind of academic reform; because rising rates of teen suicide, child abuse, and crime are often linked to the quality of parenting; because we are approaching a time when fatherlessness is as common as fatherhood.

For many kids, the network of adult role models, moms and dads in the neighborhood, uncles, aunts, and grandparents is gone—and not just for poor kids.

Why should the public schools be involved in family issues? Because, like it or not, they're still the only common portal through which most American youngsters pass. Yet today, except for an occasional home economics or child-development class (always electives), talking about family issues is more of a taboo than talking about sex. And boys rarely enroll in such electives.

Why don't schools do more than they already do? Three reasons.

1. *Money.* With budgets already cut to the bone, school districts are unlikely to take on one more substantial expense.

2. *College entrance requirements.* "High schools require computer literacy but not parenting literacy," says Judy Kirsten. "Consequently, school boards don't consider parenting an important course topic."

3. *Values.* Whose values? This is the toughest nut to crack. Parents are rightly concerned when public schools move too far into the values business. There's no cultural consensus on what constitutes good parenting values. But there is consensus on the natural stages of child development.

I have visited with some of the few public school programs that offer a place for kids to discuss family issues. I have watched hardened, violent street kids weep openly about the parents who beat them, about their aloneness, about the fact that there is no one and no place that they feel they can go, except that rare classroom or counselor, for help. Kirsten says that schools can't and shouldn't be doing this job alone. "Let's open this process up to the community, let's get the churches and lots of other institutions involved as partners."

Let's deal with the money issue by asking someone else to pay for the course (the YMCA, which already offers such a course, the churches, etc.). And let's ask our university systems to make parenting literacy an entrance requirement.

I asked Kirsten's boss, Luis Villegas, what he thinks about the idea of creating a community curriculum in family issues. Villegas is the San Diego School District's Instructional Team Leader for alternative education programs, including home schooling and the pregnant minor program. Villegas thinks the idea is workable, although he feels there should be some guidelines for what qualifies as a family issues course. But Villegas says the menu of participating institutions could be long and inclusive.

What about legal issues? For example, the separation of church and state.

Villegas sees no problem, because church-based courses would represent only one part of the menu and because schools would not be paying any church. Also, the legal and structural path already has been paved by districts that require students to do community service and permit home schooling.

The added benefit of this new approach to parenting is found in an African saying: It takes a village to raise a child. Through further involvement by community organizations and providing children with more positive role models, the village and its people are strengthened.

Obviously, there would be some risks. But the greater risk is to continue to ignore the need to prepare children—particularly boys—to become good parents. We must prepare them to be good breadwinners *and* nurturers. And more: We must take them with us, and build the new village.

V

The Men Who Build the Village

My son Matthew can't wait for the days I work at his preschool.

The basic idea of this co-operative preschool is that each parent is required to spend a few hours a month in the classroom as a teacher's aide. My wife and I, for example, each spend three hours a month in Matthew's classroom. Now and then we also work with the other parents to paint the classrooms or clean the yard.

It's a good deal. Co-op parents pay slightly less, and children have more adults in their lives.

I must admit that sometimes those three hours are the longest of my life. But I've learned not to glance at the clock or my watch. Instead, I focus on the kids, on washing their hands, on reading them stories, on raking the sand, on trying not to gag when they push dough up their noses.

FatherLove

Recently, I interviewed a group of my fellow co-op dads at the Unitarian Co-operative Preschool, one of only a handful of such preschools in the county in which we live. Like me, they don't exactly champ at the bit to get there.

One father said he actually dreaded co-oping. "I dread it because it disrupts my work rhythm, and I find it hard to slow down," said Scott Reed, who works as a community organizer.

"Intellectually, I know that this is good for my child and for the other kids, and for me," said another father, who works in law enforcement, "but to be honest, I wouldn't do it if it wasn't required."

At this preschool, co-oping moms outnumber co-oping dads by at least three to one.

"One of the kids asked me whose mommy I was," said one father.

Nonetheless, as another dad put it, co-oping makes us feel more three-dimensional as fathers. And perhaps as men, too.

Harn Cordua, a fifth-grade teacher, said co-oping was a relief to him. "At the school where I teach, I'm the navigator making sure all these individual vessels converge at the same point. But when I'm co-oping here, I don't have to be in control. I don't have to be onstage."

Listening to him, I thought of how I sometimes feel, sitting on the floor at the preschool, back against the wall, reading to Matthew and his friends. I swear I can feel my metabolism change; I become someone I used to be, someone with some time to, say, watch the dust fall in front of a window.

Steve Garber, a poet who owns a plumbing business, feels something, too. "There's a power that my daughter draws from me when I'm here. She's usually off playing with the other kids, but I can still feel it. And she gives me power, too."

It's important for men to spend time at preschools, said Reed, even if they don't feel comfortable or natural doing it. "One day I realized how hungry a couple of boys in my class were for the affection of a father figure. I was surprised at how much affection and compassion they drew out of me."

For members of our parents' generation, connecting with other parents and their children came naturally. They often knew the neighborhood kids. Today, because of our trans-regional life-style, school is the new neighborhood for kids, and the workplace is the new neighborhood for parents.

Co-oping helps connect these new neighborhoods.

"Co-oping makes me feel more three-dimensional because my daughter will come home and talk about her relationship with this child or that child, and they're not just names," said Steve Weber.

Over the past three years, I've come to know Matthew's neighborhood and Matthew's friends.

A tiny, quiet girl who has "Santa Claus hair," as my son announced one day, has grown strong of heart and mind and can climb higher than all the boys.

A boy prone to tears now comes dressed in superhero costumes that his mother has painstakingly sewn, and he cries less.

The largest and toughest boy, once the Master of the Universe on his Big Wheel trike, now cries at the smallest slight; the nearest adult will hold him until the Master of the Universe, who has become more likable, reemerges.

I have seen my son and these children grow together, become part of one another, like saplings whose branches spread and touch.

Their parents also connect. It's not comfortable asking

for advice or insight from another parent. But when you're leaning on a broom, watching the kids tumble across the sand like fall leaves, it's somehow easier to reach out.

"At work, my male friends don't talk much about their kids; they talk about their golf scores," said Weber. He wants more. "Pretty soon it won't be cool for my daughter to hang around with her dad. I don't want to look back with regret that I didn't spend enough time with her. That's what I'm hanging on to now."

Men often express their hunger to feel more three-dimensional as dads; they yearn for something beyond today's limited definition of father as breadwinner or even nurturer. When pressed in conversation, they describe something larger, a dimension of fathering inclusive of breadwinning and nurturing, but larger—the weaving of a web of support for families: community-building, village-making. The third dimension includes but extends beyond work and the home; it envelops the community of children and the community of parents. This third dimension of fatherlove is a union of two parts: first is the degree to which fathers are capable of reaching out to other parents, especially other fathers, to gain and to give support; the second aspect is our involvement beyond the home in the neighborhood, in the wider community, and how that involvement helps shape our children and makes them safer.

Fathers start from a deficit. Whether working in the home or mothering while holding down a career, women are still far more likely than men to volunteer in the schools, to make connections with one another in the workplace, to turn to one another for emotional support and help.

In recent decades men have withdrawn from their roles as neighborhood protectors; many value community less than their fathers and grandfathers did. According to the Massachusetts Mutual Life Insurance study, 44 percent of Americans believe that today's fathers are not doing as well as in the past at the most basic element of community-building: showing respect for others.

Men's withdrawal from the wider community can be seen as an extension of their withdrawal from family. At the extreme of this disintegration is the inner city, where marriage has become a relative rarity as homicide has become the leading killer of young men. These trends are not unrelated.

"It's not just the absence of a stable adult male figure from a single household that does so much damage in these communities," Mercer Sullivan, a research associate at the New School for Social Research in New York, told the *Washington Post* in 1991. Sullivan has been studying the inner city for thirty years. "At the neighborhood level, when you have lots of households where fathers are not present, the whole social order breaks down. Teenagers take over the streets."[69]

They take over the streets and turn to peers and gangs to provide their sense of connection, of initiation, of fatherhood.

We should not, however, hold only men responsible for the breakdown of the web because so many of them have deserted the community, no more than we should hold women responsible for it because they have chosen to work outside the home and neighborhood.

The wider community has also deserted parents. "The blame is not to be laid at women's doors or at men's," writes Prof. Edward Zigler of Yale. "If there is a failure of ethos, perhaps it derives from a waning of the sense of community—a declining sense of the responsibilities that made up some of the meaning of family life for Americans. . . . The larger society no longer has a unified code of values."[70]

Ray Oldenburg, author of *The Great Good Place,* a fine book about disappearing community, writes that the problem is not entirely with a husband and father who is shirking his duty: "The problem stems from the loss of that concerned and helpful contingent of *other* adults who helped raise children and who had earlier lent continuous social support to the nuclear but far from isolated family unit of the past."[71]

It takes an entire village to raise a child. But in the age of MTV and microchips, where do we find the village? And if we cannot find it, how do we build it?

Mothers and fathers are isolated in the culture, closed in by their fear of being seen as second-class employees because they have family duties and are often overstressed by long commutes. Fathers, in particular, have narrowed their universe to the workplace and the television.

Many mothers who now face the added exhaustion of careers, in addition to household responsibilities, feel nearly as disconnected from community as men—although women have more of a cultural memory of what it is like to help and be helped by other parents, and they tend to be more assertive about reaching out than men.

In coming years men may begin to reclaim their stake in the wider community, in the neighborhood, the school, the preschool. The reasons for this reawakening range from the fact that so many men are feeling lonely to the fact that men are, often, no longer the sole or main breadwinners within their families; to express themselves, to feel potent, they may reach beyond work, beyond their house, in ways they may find surprisingly fulfilling, and oddly, perhaps genetically, familiar.

The rebuilding of community starts at a very personal level.

Many men today are confronting their own sense of loneliness and disconnection from their families, from the places in which they live.

A few days ago, on a work trip, I was met at the airport by a good friend. We were crossing a bridge over a bay, talking, watching the ships move out across the silver water. As usual, we talked about our work. But then the conversation shifted to a subject we seldom share. He is the father of a young woman in her twenties. He is among the best, most thoughtful fathers I know, and yet he sometimes suffers regret and paralysis when he thinks about his fathering:

"I'm not sure what to say this is, but there is something out there that is so overwhelming. . . . It's a great weight. It's like a black blanket. No matter how much I try to get out from under it, try to kick it off, it's too heavy."

Men often have this feeling of pessimism, he added. "We don't know what it is. We can define parts of it: I've got to make money; I have trouble relating to my wife; the TV news is so grim I can't respond. Part of it is how powerless I feel when it comes to education and homelessness and drugs. There are all kinds of things that make up this blanket."

Women describe this blanket as well: they see men pushing around beneath it; they hear them sweating and groaning and sometimes whining about it, and at some level this angers women, or at least many of the women I have interviewed. It angers my wife. It irritates her because as a nurse she is trained to fix things. Also, as a mother and daughter, she is trained to care for others, to be cheerful, to be a caregiver. But when she sees me under that blanket for too long she resists the urge to rip it off because she knows that, like my friend, I am sometimes more comfortable beneath the weight of this blanket than I will admit. So are many of the men I have met.

This blanket can be a convenient shield, can't it? It can protect us from being brave, from confrontation, from economic risk, from chores, from bosses who are too much like our fathers or not enough like our fathers. It protects us from our wives. In a curious way, it protects us from our manhood, and most tragically, it protects us from our children.

A man who cuts himself off from community, from friends, particularly male friends, also at some level cuts himself off from his own family. Many of the good men that I interviewed said they felt deadened after a while, from focusing on bringing home the bacon and cooking it, too. The wisest fathers, like my friend who described the blanket, do not suggest that anyone should pity them for feeling deadened (an oppression and fatigue shared now by many working women), but they do wish that their lives were more than a series of professional or even parental chores.

They sense, too, that one route to a wider definition of fatherhood, a wider experience, is through connecting with their male friends, especially other fathers. The unexpressed fear among women and employers and perhaps, too, among the politically powerful is that should men begin to turn to one another for some sense of connection beyond family and work, they will begin to express passion about life—and passion in the corporate world can be a dangerous thing. Particularly male passion, because it is so unexpected.

Robert Bly suggests that the most damaged part of the psyche in modern man is the "lover," the ability to love life, to feel tenderness or passion.

Modern society accepts, even applauds, a man for channeling all his attention and emotional needs and all his semblance of passion in one direction, his work. It is marginally but increasingly acceptable in our culture to widen that attention to include his wife and children. But to widen his passion further, to extend that passion toward friends and community is less acceptable, although a man cannot fully care for his family unless he also cares for the community in which he lives.

There are two aspects of this prohibition against the father's involvement in community: one is the subtle cultural restrictions on civic involvement. For example, many corporations have policies precluding employees from participating in political events or running for office. The National Civic League, based in Denver, has for the past few years been trying to challenge corporate policies against such civic-mindedness. We have reached a point in our society when politics, education, and community building is supposed to be left up to the professionals. Ironically, as women have moved into the civic arena, joining Kiwanis or Rotary, running for office, men—or at least many of the men I have interviewed—have further depressed their passion for the world, have moved deeper beneath the blanket.

The second aspect of this prohibition is the society's subtle restrictions on male friendship.

Theories abound on why, for so many men, this is so: homophobia; or the belief that men are biologically geared to competitiveness, precluding friendship. Some of the theories are suspect. What we do know is that our culture discourages deep friendships among men. As Larry Letich writes in *The Utne Reader:*

> ... Our society's ideal man is not supposed to have any emotional needs. Since few men can actually live up to that ideal, it's considered acceptable, even laudable, for him to channel all his emotional needs in one direction—his wife and children. A man who has any other important emotional bonds (that are not based on duty, such as an ailing parent) is in danger of being called neglectful, or irresponsible, or weak, because forging emotional bonds with others takes time—time that is supposed to be spent "getting ahead."
>
> Small wonder that the only friendships allowed are those that serve a "business" purpose or those that can be fit effortlessly into one's leisure time. Maintaining one's lawn is more important than maintaining one's friendships. . . .
>
> Think of the impression that comes to mind from a thousand movies and TV shows about the guy who "leaves his wife" for the evening to "go out with the guys." Invariably, the other guys are shown as both immature and lower-class, losers who'll never amount to anything in life. The message is clear—no self-respecting middle-class man hangs out regularly with his friends.[72]

My wife knows what I need. Not long ago, she conspired with my farmer-woodworker buddy, who allegedly taught me how to fly-fish. She called him up and made the arrangements for later in the spring, then told me about them on the morning of my forty-fourth birthday, when I was thinking mainly about death and taxes.

She said, "Nick will pick you up at the Albuquerque airport in his truck. You and he will drive to northern New Mexico where you and he will fish." Her tone said: This is an order.

Wonderful! I can go guilt-free. Or nearly guilt-free.

Nick and I will drive stream to stream, and I'll probably borrow a couple of his cigarettes (and not inhale) and pretend for a few days that I am a farmer-woodworker-fly-fisherman. If our trip is like others we have taken, we will devise a new foreign policy, or at least try to agree on one, and we will also talk about our fathering.

The last time we did this, we took a break from fishing to climb a mountain. Winding up through groves of aspen, we got into a tense discussion about disciplining our children. By the time we got to the top, we were silent, and we sat on a log and ate our sandwiches and didn't say anything more about our philosophical disagreement about parenting; it was easier to devise foreign policy.

While interviewing one group of mothers, several wondered why men don't talk more with one another about their fathering. The answer, it seems to me, is that we do talk about fathering, but we do it differently from women. We do it indirectly, between the lines.

All generalizations are wrong, if not sexist, but let me wade on.

We men should put ourselves in harm's way more often; we should get away from the office and the television and spend more time with our male friends, and we should allow the topic of fathering to surface.

The women in the group were puzzled that this seems so hard for men.

"We're not prohibiting them from being friends; they are," said one mom. "My husband gets together with his friends, and they go hiking, but he always ends up getting bummed out because there is this competition that develops between the friends; they always end up talking about business and how much money they make, or how great their business is doing. None of these guys will admit how hard their work is or how lousy their business is really doing, let alone how hard fathering is."

Another woman said, "I have a group of friends from college; I take a trip every year with just these six women. We've gone someplace interesting every year for four or five years. And every time I have taken my trip, I have said to my husband, 'Why don't you go up to San Francisco after I come back and see your friend Ken?' And he doesn't do it. He'll say, 'No, I don't think I could make it without you guys,' meaning our little nuclear family. Why is that?"

Whatever the reason for men's reticence to talk to one another about fathering, they need to talk to somebody about it.

One woman said her husband loves going to a parenting group. "This is the one time he feels that he has permission to sit there and wallow in being a dad," she said. "He can just let it out; he can get specific. In normal settings, men just don't tend to get that specific. I just can't imagine men having a power lunch and one of them saying, 'Hey, what do you do when your kid picks her nose all the time?' "

I haven't seen any studies suggesting that male friendship is a prerequisite for good fathering, but it couldn't hurt. Who knows most what it's really like to be a father than a man who happens to be a father? Maybe men do need a little encouragement from women, and from each other.

"My husband, who is a psychiatrist, would probably be lost if he couldn't talk about being a father with his friends," said one mother, who successfully encourages her husband to take time off in the company of his male friends. "Every year he takes his male-bonding trip with a friend. They'll go off to Nepal, Peru, Ecuador, and they just talk about fatherhood and their lives and their work. Being a psych nurse, I know a lot of psychiatrists who aren't nearly that open about their emotions. My husband's trips are hard physically, but his work is hard emotionally; so when he comes back, things seem to have fallen into place for him; he'll be in balance."

New Mexico isn't Nepal, Peru, or Ecuador, but it's far enough for me. I'm looking forward to seeing Nick. I have thought about our discussion about disciplining our children ever since our last trip, and perhaps, while trudging up a mountain or wading the San Juan, we will pick up where we left off.

I am purposefully mixing the subjects of male friendship, family, and the building of community. These subjects are too often segregated, as if one of these can exist in health without the others. It makes as much sense to segregate the issues of friendship and community from family as it does to segregate family life from the workplace and the pressures the workplace puts on families.

In order to find our way back to a stronger sense of fatherhood, we must take a circuitous route—through our friends, through other fathers, through our community. Without a stronger web of connections beyond the home, the family is endangered. Parents do not, *cannot*, parent alone. Increasingly we sense that in order to be true fathermen, we must rediscover an ancient truth about fatherlove.

We are the protectors of the nest. At the very least, we are full partners with women in protecting our nests. We can protect our nests best by becoming passionately involved in building a stronger community around our nests, taking our children with us into the community and teaching them by our example that no one parents alone.

Once the loneliness and sense of disconnectedness is recognized, the first step toward becoming keepers of the village is to *act,* to reach out to other fathers, and also to mothers. Let me clarify here that I am not describing some New Age Grok. This reconnection with other fathers, and with a wider community, can be made simply, through, for example, the accidental connection with fathers that my fellow co-opers and I feel at the preschool. Connection, village-building, can also take place in the most traditional of ways.

"Soccer saved my life," says John Holtkamp, a forty-year old social worker and former single father. Before he explains the Zen of soccer, he describes the rural community in which he was born and raised, the roots and connections that so many of us have lost.

"All the support systems were there," he says. "In Lee County, Iowa, many of us were related. Someone did a family tree and found that old Gerhart Johann Holtkamp, who came here in 1836, has three thousand living descendants. I knew the family history of almost everybody in the county."

Extended family was more than just a sociological concept. One relative, whose father was a brutal alcoholic and whose mother had committed suicide, was taken in by Holtkamp's large family. "That's called foster care today." Grandma came by when the new babies were born; Aunt Lucille was available to provide baby-sitting at a moment's notice. "My wife and I had all those advantages when we started having kids."

In 1987 Holtkamp and his wife separated. He got a new

job and moved to Des Moines with his four children, to a neighborhood where kids were the exception.

"A lawyer lived next door. He and his wife drove a BMW, lived in a nice brick home. They had this little baby who had everything, and the baby was being treated like a small, exotic pet. Here I was with these four children. Maybe it was just paranoia, but I felt as if they were looking at me and wondering, 'Hasn't he figured out where kids come from?' "

Holtkamp's kids had no one in the neighborhood to play with. Like many single parents, he knew no one with whom he could share parenting problems. After years of not worrying about child care, he watched most of his $8,000 in savings disappear in a single year to day-care bills.

"I suddenly understood all the rhetoric I had heard from women about the need for good, affordable child care, which is a contradiction in terms." The demands of his job grew. "I wasn't able to get the job done. I would bring work home, get the children settled down. I know there were bright colors in the world during that year in my life, but my memory of that time is all gray."

His routine became mechanical. He would help his kids with homework, make supper, wrangle the kids into bed, spread out his work on the table, and work until midnight every night. "There were times when I found myself at eleven at night, looking at the papers spread over the table with tears running down my face, just thinking, 'How am I going to hold this together?' " One of his sons needed extensive surgery at the University of Iowa. "I was making arrangements for the other children, and . . ."

At this point in his story, Holtkamp pauses for a long moment.

"All the pieces of our lives couldn't be put together. The

children would say, 'Dad, you're not fun anymore,' 'Dad, how come we don't do anything in the evenings?' 'Dad, how come you don't talk that much anymore?' "

After a year's separation, he and his wife reunited. His experience as a single parent had opened his eyes to the world beyond work, to the demands of being a nurturing parent, and the isolation that sometimes accompanies it.

He and his family moved to a new housing development with lots of kids. At first he believed that his sense of isolation was over. But slowly he realized that much of the web of support he had experienced growing up in small-town Iowa and during his early years of marriage did not exist in this suburb either.

"Here I was, a supposedly professional social worker, and I didn't know how to become a part of a neighborhood, what the key was."

A month after Holtkamp moved to the neighborhood, a stranger knocked on the door. Loren Birchmier, standing on the doorstep, introduced himself. Birchmier said he lived in an adjacent housing tract. He was recruiting kids for new soccer teams, and he was looking for dads who might want to become coaches.

"I'll be forever grateful to Loren," says Holtkamp today. "Here was my invitation into the fraternity of fathers in that neighborhood."

In recent decades, mothers had a number of mechanisms to connect with other mothers—coffee klatches, park benches, connecting with other mothers through school or their children's friends. More recently, mothers' support groups have sprung up in neighborhoods and churches. Or mothers form informal groups at the office. They share parenting skills, commiserate over the pressures of parenting, and plan community activities.

Today many men are also beginning to experience the

rewards of turning to fellow parents, particularly other fathers, for expertise and support.

As a new soccer coach, Holtkamp was swept up into a world of dads and kids. "Suddenly the paperwork on my desk at work didn't seem so vital if I had ten little five- or six-year-old guys waiting for the coach to show up. So I wasn't staying at work as late anymore. Soccer forced me home, forced me to interact with my kids. I felt energized again. I'd get home after soccer and go out in back with the kids and kick the ball around or play some basketball."

Soccer also helped Holtkamp connect with other parents. As the five-year-olds raced across the grass, he found himself turning to his fellow soccer coaches for parenting information, even though the connection was indirect, oblique.

"A person's extended family, which is probably spread out across the country, tends to give you *direct* advice," says Holtkamp. "But implicit in the act of giving advice is the assessment that you *need* advice, which can be subtly interpreted as 'You may not know what you're doing as a parent.' Of course, I've moved before, and I'll move again, and my extended family will always be needed. But for now, I have more frequent contact with the soccer coaches."

Tom Hay, one of Holtkamp's fellow coaches, says that soccer is about the only place he speaks freely about child rearing with other men. "I work at a tire factory," says Hay, thirty-three. "A lot of the guys at work sit around at lunch and talk about sports, work, everything except parenting. Sometimes we'll talk about our kids' achievements, what they've done right. But we don't talk about our kids if they've done something wrong or if we're having difficulty as parents. At work, we don't ask each other for help."

Hay and Holtkamp agree that the dynamics of the soccer field help them open up.

"We give each other hints," Hay explains. "It's not like you tell someone, 'Hey, you should ease up on your kid.' It's more like you approach the subject sideways. You say, 'You know, one time I was getting on my kids' case all the time, and I tried approaching the problem this way.' Maybe that helps the dad start talking about the issue he's facing with his boy. Or maybe he just listens."

Another of Holtkamp's fellow coaches is Ted Bzdega, an at-home dad mentioned earlier. Bzdega, a woodworker, is responsible for most of the domestic duties in his household.

"In addition to talking with dads on the soccer field, I find I like talking to at-home moms," he says. "I get the sense from them that little moments in life are the most important. That's something men can miss if they're always obsessing about the big picture."

For many men, oblique communication, which often accompanies sports, is more comfortable than the more direct and open approach psychologists say may often come easier to women. Men tend to communicate with other men by sharing activities—by doing rather than talking. Perhaps primitive male hunters communicated, by necessity, with as few words as possible; women, more likely to be sharing domestic duties in the village, found it more appropriate to speak directly and often.

As the division of labor between men and women continues to blur, we may need to move away from such a stark division in communication styles. Nonetheless, the subtle soccer connection has great value to these men, and they find themselves opening up to other possibilities.

Rick Carnahan, who works at a Des Moines feed store, says that he has watched with admiration as John Holtkamp's competitiveness and tension have softened. "John's more sensitive than when we first started. Like the rest of us, he's realized soccer is like life. Some losses. Some gains."

Holtkamp admits to an occasional excess of zeal. "Sometimes I catch myself yelling too harshly, 'Are you in this play? C'mon!' It's hard sometimes to turn the work switch off when I'm coaching. Sometimes I'm too competitive. I need to watch that."

"Coaching gets kind of demanding," says Carnahan. He says his normal tendency would be to stay home and watch TV, but soccer forces him out into the community of kids and parents. "I mow the soccer field, go to all the tournaments, go out to eat with groups of parents who have kids on the team."

Like many men, Holtkamp wouldn't be caught dead in a men's group, pounding drums or baring his chest and soul. Nonetheless, he is moved by the other coaches who subtly guide him in his fathering, and he's learning to return the favor.

Of course, soccer coaching isn't the only way fathers can connect with other parents while participating in kids' activities. The dad connection can occur in father-child church programs or PTA activities.

An increasing number of dads enjoy such programs as Y-Indian Guides, originated by the YMCA in the 1920s for fathers and sons ages five through eight. This program, which is experiencing a boom in membership, focuses on strengthening the bond between parent and child while teaching children about Native American culture. Unlike the Boy Scouts, fathers are required to attend every meeting and camp out with their children. (Similar YMCA programs now exist for fathers and daughters, mothers and sons, and other family configurations.) As with soccer, fathers comment that being an Indian Guide not only forces them to carve out time for their children, but also to bond with other dads.

Sometimes all we have to do is remember where we came from.

The village, this sense of community and friendship, can assemble in small, informal ways, as it has for Andre Duplessis and other African-American men who live in different parts of San Diego and live at different economic levels. They are linked through church work and a card game called bid whist, which Duplessis calls "the black man's bridge."

"We're playing it again," says Duplessis, who is thirty-seven and sells advertising for a living. Twelve years into his second marriage, he is the father of seven children and a grandfather. He says he's trying to raise his children in the community of the church, but when he talks about bid whist his eyes light up.

For a while, he says, the art was lost, but for the past five years, these parents have been getting together after church to play the game. "The parents get together, and we have a potluck, and we talk about the kids while we're playing bid whist and the kids are playing around us," says one of the men. He says this "village," at the church and at the card table, is growing. During the week, the parents will call each other up to "help each other through the struggles of life," says another man.

Duplessis' roots are in New Orleans; during the mass migration in the late forties, his parents moved to Southern California. "They had bid whist clubs and got together the same way we do now," says Duplessis.

During the summers, his parents would pack the kids up and return, by road or by train, to New Orleans, and the family would join the families of their roots. On Friday evening, the men would go out on the Gulf of Mexico in small boats to catch fish, and the women would stay behind, prepare the seasoning and the fixings, and wait for the men to come back. While they were waiting, the women would play tonk, which is similar to gin rummy. The kids would play at their feet. Then the men would come back with the fish, and the families would feast and play bid whist.

Sharon Griffin, an African-American journalist, tells me that she, too, grew up at the feet of a community of parents who played bid whist. Raised in North Carolina, some of her best memories are of these times, when the men would team up against the women, and the home of the bid whist host would rumble with the pounding of small feet and laughing children. As part of the ritual of the game, the players would outdo each other with tall tales. "I was so poor that I only had one pair of pants," one dad would say and slap a card down. "Well, my brother and I were so poor we had to share a pair of pants, so we traded off going to school every other day." *Slap.*

Recently, Griffin, who helps an organization that resettles African refugees, overheard a conversation among Ugandan refugees, and one of the men said, "My family was so poor we only owned one pair of pants . . ."

Much of African-American culture, she believes, is more rooted in communal memories than we may realize. She remembers as a child listening to the stories of her parents and their friends, learning how they had overcome past struggles as they slapped the cards down. She remembers how she felt then: cared for by all the adults around the table. She remembers playing until exhausted and sleeping beneath a blanket of snapping cards and murmuring voices.

FatherLove

Listening to Griffin and Duplessis and the others describe bid whist, I wondered about the cultural differences of card playing. In the culture in which I grew up, there were tasteful ladies' bridge clubs or men's night out: cigars, beer, and no kids or women allowed.

Perhaps there are other communal card cultures, ones that include children, in Anglo society. If not, perhaps there should be. Duplessis and the others describe bid whist as one of the arts of parenting, of village making, and they are glad that they have found it again. As fathers, it connects them to each other; it also connects them to mothers and children.

The second step toward village building is for men to confront just how physically and emotionally isolating so many of our cities and suburbs have become and to do something about it.

After the Industrial Revolution, women became the lasting glue that held the web of social connections together in the schools and neighborhood and village. They were the ones who knew the neighborhood, the ones who raised money for community centers, made sure the parks were safe and well equipped. Even during the 1950s and early 1960s, there was more sense of place; women usually felt this more keenly than men because they usually spent more hours in the neighborhood, but men were often there, too, in the front lawn, with their water hoses. I can remember how my father spent time in the yard watering, puttering, talking with the man next door. Some spring nights all the fathers would be standing at the ends of the driveways, observing the clouds during tornado watches.

But slowly men became divorced from their neighborhoods, cut off from much connection to the fabric in which our homes were held. Today, many women, too, have moved into the workplace and away from the neighborhood.

Dripping from the shower, Mom slaps sandwiches together. Dad stumbles through the house to the drip-grind. Mom roars off with Mikey to a day care ten or fifteen miles away, then drives eighteen miles in the opposite direction to work. Dad jams Lenny and Missy (and accidentally, Offense the cat) into the Volvo and heads for the magnet school twelve miles to the south, where Missy spends her days. He drops Lenny at the school bus stop; Lenny will ride the bus forty-five minutes to another magnet school. Then Dad drives to another county, where he puts in a twelve-hour day.

Year after year, members of this family are scattered like circling planets that periodically cross paths, then start the same whirling all over again. They grab moments of time and find meaning in them, but yearn for dreamtime.

Maybe this three-decade experiment in trans-regional living is driving us crazy. At best it's a pretty inefficient way to structure our lives. Such a life-style doesn't leave much time to get to know our neighbors or our children's teachers, or feel any sense of attachment to a place. Social scientists and urban experts once showed some interest in the implications of workers commuting long distance. But the interest has faded. Meanwhile, Dad commuting long distance turned into Dad, Mom, Mikey, Lenny, and Missy commuting long distances, leading these fragmented lives.

What are the effects of this strange explosion, this hurtling outward that families go through every weekday and even on the weekends? (Lenny and Missy no longer go to school with the neighborhood kids—possibly don't even know them. Mom or Dad drives them to play dates miles away.)

FatherLove

"I haven't seen any studies on that," says Bob Dunphy, senior researcher at the Urban Land Institute and an expert on commuting patterns. "But a recent study done for the U.S. Department of Transportation shows that commuting distances have substantially increased—about twenty-five percent—over the past seven years."

Apparently, people are voting with their odometers.

"People are always willing to trade a longer commute for a perceived improvement in their quality of life," says William Fulton, editor of *California Planning and Development Report*. In California they define that as seclusion, segregation, walling off the outside world, even though the safety may be illusion. People feel they have to make these choices for their children, but I'd like to know what the impact is of two generations of kids going everywhere via car pool, being totally dependent on adults."

We study how, say, secondary smoke affects our lungs; we can turn to scientific studies to help us make decisions about smoking in the workplace. City planners who route sewage think about health questions; surely they would think about how trans-regional living affects health.

Despite the changes in our life-style, our hunger for community has not disappeared.

When David Pijawka set out to study Phoenix's neighborhoods, he pretty much bought the conventional academic wisdom that neighborhoods are dead—particularly in new, sprawling Phoenix, which until recently didn't have many real neighborhoods. Pijawka is an associate professor of environmental geography at Arizona State University. Over the past year, Pijawka and his students asked Phoenicians to identify their neighborhoods and tell what they valued about them.

The most unexpected finding, according to Pijawka, was how highly people ranked the importance of neighbor-

149

hoods to their social life. "We really believed that this would come out at the bottom of the list, but it came out surprisingly high," he says. "This wasn't true for all neighborhoods. For example, the residents in a strong, old neighborhood didn't really consider a lot of socializing with their neighbors to be all that important. They took for granted the friendliness of their neighborhood. As we approach the twenty-first century, people are expressing real concern that the urban experience of the sixties and seventies has not worked out, that the cost of regional living on family life is too high, and that somehow we've got to move back to neighborhoods," says Pijawka. "One building block you can start with is the protection of children."

This is already a rediscovered frontier for some men. At schools and in neighborhoods around the country, a few good men are challenging one another to take a hand in their children's physical safety.

For example, at San Diego's Sherman Elementary School, a crew of parents, primarily fathers, cut back bushes in a nearby vacant lot that drug abusers used as a shooting gallery. Sherman teachers and parents also established a school Neighborhood Watch. Signs were placed all around the school; homes that face Sherman now sport School Watch signs, and the school employees and students keep an eye on the surrounding homes.

Similarly, fathers of students at Arlington High in Indianapolis created Security Dads in 1991. Many of Arlington's students came from poor neighborhoods, and a third of the 1,650 students were being raised by single parents. Large school events—pep rallies, dances—were consistently disruptive and dangerous; like many urban schools, Arlington High students were confronted by gangs and guns. So principal Jacqueline Greenwood asked parents to help. At first, she turned to the mothers, but she soon decided that mothers were not going to be able to control tough adolescent boys. A school nurse bought her husband a T-shirt decorated in the school colors, with the slogan "Security Dad" printed on the back, and asked him to help patrol the school. Other fathers joined, often because their children asked them to.

Security Dads ride buses to and from sporting events or on field trips; the school now can hold dances and other after-school events. Students say that they prefer having the fathers around instead of security guards. The program has had three benefits: added security; a male presence in the lives of the students whose fathers aren't around; and the fulfillment of a traditional male role that fathers have avoided, or from which they have been excluded or excused.

At one game, a gang-related shooting erupted. Anthony Wallace, the first Security Dad, took charge, protecting his students, controlling their panic. Linda Wallace, his wife, told *Parade* magazine, "My husband was in tears when he got home. He's not that type of person, but he was so moved that the kids did what he said without him having to yell. They knew he cared, that he was their friend, and they responded."

Her husband added, "What guy wants to go to some PTA meeting and hear a bunch of women talk? But give us something we can do, where we're really needed, and we'll be there."[73]

Fatherlove is essential to every school community.

Some of this male presence must be created by school districts. They must make a greater effort to hire male teachers, particularly at the elementary school level. Schools could also offer more support to fathers who may choose to home-school their children. The vast majority of home-schooling parents are mothers, but that proportion could change as the job market changes. A man who is out of work for an extended period might, in fact, discover a new male identity as a home-school teacher to his children.

Ultimately, much of the infusion of fatherlove in schools must come from dads who volunteer their time. Helping with the physical improvement of schools, through community involvement, may be one area where fathers feel particularly comfortable. Dads did at Torrey Pines Elementary in upper-class Del Mar, California. Principal Dennis Doyle had a problem. His school's outdoor lunch court had no covering to shelter students from ultraviolet rays. He asked the San Diego school system to build a screen. School district officials responded with an estimate of $40,000 and said that the money would have to come out of Doyle's school's strained budget. Doyle asked parents to help. They raised money, and fathers who were contractors built the shelter for $2,000.

Parents and teachers at my son's elementary school were fed up that their children's school had not been painted, inside or out, since the 1960s. So the parents and teachers formed a vigilante painting party. When my son and I arrived at Oak Park's painting party, the hallway buzzed with happy teachers, parents, and students. Here was the sense of community that many of us, particularly fathers, didn't often experience. At the time, my son, who is bused to this school, was feeling like the new kid on the block. But on the day of the painting party, he led me to door of his room and announced that he wanted to scrape that door first.

After that day, he felt that he owned a piece of that school. And so did I.

Fathers are also potent figures in the classroom, as volunteer aides or speakers. Such visits by both parents, but perhaps especially fathers (if for no other reason than the relative scarcity of men in schools), can make a dramatic difference in the academic life of their own child, and other children as well. A Stanford University study designed to isolate those factors that could improve a child's grades, independent of socioeconomic standing, found that if a child's parent makes at least one visit to the school during the year, that child's grades are likely to improve. The visit convinces the child that his or her parents care about school, and communication is improved between the teacher and the parent.[74]

A little bit can go a long way. Among my most vivid memories of my own father is of the day he came to my second grade class. As an engineer, he had been asked by the teacher to come to explain the atomic bomb. My memory is bright and detailed: he is sitting on one of those little elementary school chairs, knees together, hat in hand, waiting. . . .

Volunteering in schools is only one method of village-building for men. Kimbrall suggests that the men's movement work to strengthen community-based boys' clubs, scout troops, sports leagues, as well as big brother programs, which help fatherless male children find self-esteem through positive role models.

All of the institutions and organizations that involve parents or children should examine how their assumptions and language exclude or excuse men from participation. For example, in Colorado the director of a community center for parents told why the name of the center was changed. "For eight years, we were called the Mother Center. We changed it to the Parents' Center. Right away we had dads with their toddlers taking part in the support groups. We had dads writing editorials for us. We had dads on the board. One guy showed up at a potluck with this contraption that looked like like a steam engine; it was a barbeque smoker, and he smoked all this meat for everybody. He was the provider of the meat. That's the first time he came, and he kept on coming."

While a name and attitude adjustment may not, in all cases, be so immediately productive, it's a good place to start.

As an aspect of psychological village-building, fathers may have a special role in extending their children's physical, psychological, and intellectual boundaries, and by doing so, extend their own sense of fatherhood.

David Mollering is the divorced father of a nine-year-old daughter. He shares custody of Emily with his wife. Once, I told David how I walked in my neighborhood with my sons, particularly at night. David and I discussed how odd it was that when we were kids, and when our parents were kids, everybody knew their neighborhoods, but the children knew the neighborhoods—the nooks and crannies and alleys and dogs—better than any adult. Now we find ourselves, as fathers, introducing our children to the neighborhood. We agreed that doing so was often a surprisingly wonderful adventure, particularly at night.

David told me this story:

Last night, I didn't want to sit down with Emily after dinner and watch TV. I hadn't seen her since Thursday, so we went for a walk. It was great. Nobody seems to go out walking at night in the neighborhood anymore. We were the only people out. She held my hand the whole time. I grew up in this neighborhood. We walked through the alleys where I used to play guns and play fort and hide and seek. If we had taken our walk during the day she wouldn't have held my hand. There would have been distractions and cars. She wondered what it would be like if she grows up and has kids, and maybe raises them in this neighborhood, too. She asked me what it was like, when I was a child, to have all my friends in the same neighborhood. She doesn't have that. We have to drive her somewhere. She said, "I'm scared." I told her how the alleys bothered me when I was a kid with a paper route. She's usually scared of the dark. But the fear last night was good; it was part of the edge: We both started chattering away. In another few years, she won't talk to me like this.

David wondered why he and Emily did not go for more walks in the neighborhood. Maybe, he said, it was because television flooded children's and adults' minds with so many negative and violent images. (Indeed, studies at the Annenberg School of Communication show that families who watch a lot of television believe their neighborhoods are even more dangerous than they are.) David said he planned to walk in his neighborhood more with his daughter, and he talked about what he thought this intimate and adventurous introduction to community would teach Emily:

Besides overcoming her fear of the dark, it will help us get to know each other better. Maybe part of what fathers do is help their kids with fear, out there, out in the world. She's not scared with me because I'm a man. I'm going to walk with her more, try to do it a couple nights a week. I want us to talk more. And I don't want her to be scared of the neighborhood.

Donald Brandes, the man described earlier who had divorced his company, tells this story about how he takes his son with him into the world of men, to an integrated club that allows women, but probably without enthusiasm:

Andrew and I joined a club. It's an old farts' club, an 1800s club, it has everything, and God, I love going with Andrew. I don't know why it is, but I love going there, and he loves going there. And we have our locker, and our names are on our locker. We change our clothes and put on our swimming trunks. Andrew's going to be five on June 27. We'll shower down, and we'll go swimming, or we'll go jogging, or we'll run around and play basketball. We'll come back in and take our showers, we'll come back to the locker, and I've got my little kiddy pack, my pack of toiletries. He'll take it, he'll get up on the stool and take out the toiletries. He'll be naked and walk back to the area where they've got all the shaving cream and shaving lotions and stuff. It's his place. We'll dry his hair—he's just a little fart, you know, but it's his place. And he's with other men, and these grandfathers look at Andrew and me getting dressed and they'll say, "Fine-looking son you've got there," and they'll raise their eyebrows. Andrew will walk away somewhere, and they'll say, "Make sure you enjoy these days with him, make sure you enjoy these times with him."

When writer Elvira Valenzuela Crocker interviewed ten leaders of the Mexican-American Women's National Organization, she found a common denominator in their backgrounds. Their fathers had made a conscious effort to introduce them to the idea of community and to take them even beyond the neighborhood, to the wider world. "What they say about their fathers," Cocker writes, "is particularly instructive to men struggling to fill those roles for today's daughters."

These are women of achievement, she writes, who excelled academically and professionally and were highly involved in their communities. They speak of how their fathers loved them and were a strong presence in their lives, whether the fathers were in the household or divorced. They spoke of fathers with high expectations of their daughters, and fathers dedicated to their communities. These fathers, mostly working class, all had strong mates, and they shared nontraditional views about what their daughters could or should do.

"My father would make a point of taking me to baseball games, even though I had two brothers who were always eager to go. I wasn't crazy about baseball. It was as if he were making a point to me and to them that there should be no stereotypes about the roles men and women play," one woman said. Gloria Barajas, coordinator of women's leadership training at the National Education Association in Washington, D.C., told how her father took her target shooting, hunting, and involved her in many other activities that boys generally do with their fathers. "As a result, I had experiences and freedom that developed my self-confidence. I learned at an early age that girls can do a lot of things that boys can do." Blandina Cardenas Ramirez, who directs the Office of Minority Concerns for the Washington-based American Council on Education, described the importance of girlhood political discussions with her father *and his circle of friends*. These formative moments, when her future opinions were encouraged and respected, remain among her cherished memories.[75]

For a father, taking a child into the third dimension can

be a joyful adventure. We have the opportunity to introduce our children to the world of adults, to our neighborhoods, our workplaces, our cities and beyond—to help our children see their environment through our eyes, and to allow them to show us our world anew through their eyes.

From the bus window, my son and I could see the skeleton of the world, the old globe of steel from the 1964 World's Fair, overgrown and empty. Once, I had stood beneath it with my own father and looked up through it to the clouds. As Jason and I passed the globe, it became a blur behind the trees, clicking past like an old home movie, disappearing. The city was ahead, spires hidden in the clouds.

"That looks like the largest graveyard in the world," said Jason.

The bus moved past the rotten hulks of abandoned cars and into New York City.

Because I have been traveling a good deal lately, I am taking the advice of friends, other parents who also travel as part of their jobs: Take your children with you whenever you can.

We checked into the Mayflower Hotel and then took a walk in the evening. Jason had his comic books with him. He is at the age when the world of comic books seems more interesting, perhaps more real, than the one outside the pages. I attempted reason.

"Here's the deal, Jason. We're in New York. If you keep your eyes open, you'll see things weirder here than anything you'll find in a comic book."

Walking beside me, he remained politely noncommittal. What Jason saw that night was stranger than a leaping

X-Man. He watched a reasonably dressed man, standing on Columbus Avenue across from the Metropolitan Opera House, singing a booming operatic tune to the opera house. He sang convincingly, arms stretched wide, chin up. The sidewalk was jammed with outdoor café patrons and evening walkers. I recalled the song, "I Like New York in June. . . ."

"Look how happy everybody is, Jason."

"Yup." He smiled.

Street vendors lined the sidewalk, and every block or so a vendor was selling used and remaindered (and possibly stolen) books. I was astonished, and then ambivalent, to find on one of the tables a copy of a book I had written.

The next day, in a cab on the way to an appointment, Jason had his nose in a comic book, "The Uncanny X-Men."

"You're going to get carsick, Jason," I warned him. The cab was gyrating through traffic. "Remember, keep your eyes open."

A few blocks later Jason said, "Dad, I just saw something." I was distracted. "Dad?"

"What?"

"I just saw somebody praying."

"OK."

"He was praying to a poster of the New Kids on the Block."

Later, after my appointment, we walked up Eighth Avenue and were momentarily swept up in a Haitian demonstration. Hundreds of cordoned-off, angry-looking people listened to a lineup of speakers. From the back of a flatbed truck, they roared out their defiance of their most recent dictator. "Keep moving," said a policeman. They were singing a beautiful, haunting anthem. Just then, Jason saw his first full-dress transvestite.

"I thought transvestites were illegal," said Jason.

"No, they're not," I said.

We moved on through the rush and crush of all the immigrants and the intelligentsia and the illiterates and the itinerants.

"By the way, where did you learn the word *transvestite?*" I asked.

Jason shrugged nonchalantly.

We were hungry. We stopped to eat at a coffee shop, and Jason confronted, on the table, an open metal bowl of large dill pickles in opaque, green juice.

"Oh, *yuck,*" he said, hands up, backing away. "That's weird."

After lunch, we arrived at the Empire State Building and looked up at the nets placed around the rim to stop the jumpers. From the top, ears popping, we looked out over the city. Visibility, according to the building's Art Deco gauge, was fifteen miles. We marveled at the roof gardens.

"There's Brooklyn. I was born there."

"In a hospital?"

"Sure. Way down there. Strange thought."

"Why?"

I couldn't really answer.

"Look!" said Jason. He pointed down.

Two balloons, one red and one orange, were wafting up toward us, and then they floated higher than we were, and a stream of air caught them and moved them across the island that is Manhattan, and they bobbed and danced in the air, on their way to balloon heaven.

I love New York in June, and now so does Jason.

FatherLove

A final challenge of the third dimension of community building is to become a political fatherman.

After reading a newspaper column I wrote about John Holtkamp and his experience as a soccer coach, I received a computer message on Compuserve, an international computer network, from Mike Kruchoski, who organizes men's movement retreats in New Mexico.

"This kooky idea that the men's movement isn't for most men really hurts us all," he wrote, "and we're advocating the idea that participants need to take what they've learned about themselves and turn it outward to benefit their families and communities. Coaching soccer is only one way to do that. We hope to explore other ways to do it well."

John Parr, president of the National Civic League, headquartered in Denver, agrees. He has begun challenging men to become politically active on behalf of their children. "Denver has been a central place for the men's movement, and many of us are frustrated with all the former political activists who have gone off to beat drums rather than make change."

Perhaps the men's movement needs a new axiom: *Real men fight for our children.*

After I mentioned this line to Parr, he began using it in Denver. "People respond to that line," he said. "A woman who heads a child-advocacy program here says she gets exhausted going to meetings and seeing mainly women. We've got to activate men."

Andrew Kimbrall agrees. "Unless we get out of the woods and start organizing, the men's movement will be the Hoola Hoop of our age," he says.

But organize for what? High on Kimbrall's list is children

and community. One reason this is so important is that, like it or not, males still command more than their fair share of power in politics, business, and civic organizations. Their absence as advocates handicaps any efforts to improve the conditions of children, of education, of how the village connects.

Male political candidates seem increasingly sterile, tongue-tied, predictable, particularly in comparison to the many vibrant women candidates in both parties. In part, this may be because men are more conditioned by the corporate and legal cultures to think about the next quarter, the bottom line, the immediate win.

Too many male politicians seem to have lost their generative instincts, their passion to create a better world not only during the next business cycle or the next political contest but for the next generation.

The father's most important political role has always been to protect his family. What constitutes political protection can be interpreted in different ways, depending on the issue or the ideology. But in today's politics, it seems to me, real men fight for children and family. That is our proper political role as father figures beyond our immediate families.

In this arena, we have a lot to learn.

The 1992 Republican convention, controlled by men, attempted to create what social historian Barbara Whitehead calls a "national kitchen table conversation" about family values; but in the process, by being so accusatory of different family configurations, some of these politicians may have damaged the national dialogue with a dreadful reductionism. The message was: children are important, but they're still women's work. On the night reserved for the full onslaught of family values, most of the speakers were women: It was a night manufactured by men, yet what it amounted to was an archaic ladies' night.

With few exceptions, men have left the political care of children up to women, along with the dishes and the laundry and the diaper changing. But the political success of women reflects the pent-up desire for political support of families. That success could be shared by men who happen to be smart politicians.

You don't have to be a candidate to be a political fatherman. In 1992 Jack Levine of Tallahassee, Florida, a former high school English teacher, organized what may be the country's most potent political effort on behalf of children. His tools are reminiscent of sixties grass-roots politics, particularly the effort to register southern black voters. The stakes today are no less urgent. Parents like Levine are beginning to rise up and say to politicians: You can't be pro-family if you're anti-parent and anti-child.

"Politicians feed us pabulum. It's the let-them-eat-values approach to politics," says Levine, director of the Florida Center for Children & Youth, a private not-for-profit citizens' organization that has launched the Florida Children's Campaign, a nonpartisan political organizing effort. "They preach to us, 'Come back to core family values,' but what they're really telling us is we're supposed to work longer, earn less, have a higher stress level in the workplace, give up even more time with our children, endure worsening health care and education for our kids."

So parents have two choices: Lie down with their kids and accept victimization, or stand up and fight back. Doing so, politically, will be a new experience for many of us. In recent decades, parents have voted even less than the general population. For example, in urban Florida's voting precincts, only two of five parenting-age citizens are registered, and only half of them voted. That means that only one in five Floridians of parenting age is involved in the electoral process. No wonder politicians think: "Where's the reward for paying attention to child care, children's health care, or education?" Or, "Where's the punishment if we don't?"

The reasons for the political disengagement of parents range from apathy to lack of education to fatigue. But the roots go deeper. Electoral laws are anti-parent and anti-child. Set by Congress, our electoral laws were originally established for a slower, small-town, neighborhood-based society. But then came sprawling urbanization, two-career marriages, and the rise in single parenting.

Today, in most states the polls are open only on Tuesday from 7:00 A.M. to 7:00 P.M. These are the hours when most parents, caught up in the trans-regional life-style, are struggling to get the kids to school or day care, are churning through a lengthening work day, commuting home, zapping the dinner in the microwave, reading a quick story to the kids, and then preparing to collapse into bed. Most parents can't vote during their lunch hour because the polling booth is an hour away. By contrast, Europeans vote on weekends; in Italy, voter turnout is typically over 90 percent, while American turnout is 50 percent and falling.

Laws governing voting times may be analogous to the literacy tests and other Jim Crow laws that kept blacks away from the polls until someone decided to do something about it.

With a little help, parents can get back into the political game. For example, Levine's campaign will soon provide child care for voters. Coordinated Child Care, a network of Florida child-care centers, has pledged to keep day-care facilities open an extra two hours on voting days so parents can be responsible citizens and still be responsible parents.

FatherLove

The real teeth of Levine's campaign, again reminiscent of the civil rights movement of the sixties, is the voter registration drive. "We're recruiting and training our own deputy voter registrars—parents, grandparents, PTA volunteers, child-care center directors," says Levine. "Wherever parents are, we'll flip down the legs of a card table and give them the chance to register to vote." In the summer and fall of 1992, the campaign established nearly a thousand voter registration sites. During six months of 1992, the campaign registered seventy thousand new voters in the state, enough political power to swing elections.

Levine has successfully recruited fathers to help with his campaign, but not enough. He has learned a bit about men's resistance to entering the political third dimension:

A man might want to go through that door, but he knows he has a fifty-fifty chance of failing on the other side, so he doesn't go. The whole test of a guy these days is: will he be seen as a winner? No one judges how you play the game; no one is kind to a loser. That's the fear that men have. It's so much easier to say no than yes. The dilemma that men face is: You can't say yes a little bit. In Florida we needed to recruit chairmen in thirty-four counties in the state. We already had an abundance of women volunteers. We needed guys, and we had to beg them. What we found was guys felt they needed one hundred percent of the facts before they'd get involved, and that they would need one hundred percent of the facts in order to go out and pitch the cause of kids. They tended to say, "Hey, I agree with you, but what if I get called on the numbers? What if I get tested? What if some newspaper reporter calls and asks me, 'Do you know all there is to know about kids?' " That's the fear that men have, that they won't know one hundred percent of the facts, and they won't win one hundred percent. But you don't have to win one hundred percent. You have to play the game. Women are more apt to just say, "I'm willing to play the game—even if I lose."

How does Levine get beyond that fear, how does he convince men to risk?

Unrefined honesty. You have to convince men to go by what they know in their gut is true about the conditions of children and the unraveling of their communities. You have to convince men that without their partnership, without their leadership, we're not going to make it. You have to tell them exactly what they can do, and you have to give them something very practical to do that uses a skill they already know and are comfortable with.

Here's a story of what worked with one man. When Levine was attempting to jump-start the children's campaign in Flagler County in Florida, among the fastest growing counties in America, this man said, "Look, I'm a real estate agent; I don't know anything about politics." But then Levine told him that the campaign needed yard signs.

"Man, if there's one thing I know, it's yard signs," said the real estate agent. "Realtors live and die by yard signs. I know where the traffic is, I know where my old customers are who would be willing to let me put the signs in their yards."

What this man was saying to Levine was: *If you let me do what I do best, and it helps kids then it's a go. Don't make me learn all this stuff about child development. Don't even bother me with the statistics. Just plug me into something I already know one hundred percent.* "He was cruising!" says Levine. "He was doing what he knew best. He became a leader."

The difference between an apolitical dad and a political fatherman is the difference between being a spectator and being on the field.

For at least two generations, manhood has been defined by how good a spectator a man was. Which team did he root for? Was his seat on the fifty-yard line, the thirty-yard line, or, God forbid, the end zone? A man was defined by how well he railed against the umpire, how well he could criticize the call. In the process, he became the guy who, at the bottom of the third martini at the airport, watched the football game on television, rather than taking an earlier flight home to be with his family. And yet, this same dad would jump in front of a car to save a kid. Says Levine:

> We tell dads, "Politics is a speeding bullet that is headed toward your kid's head, and we've got to set up a deflection." One father told me, "I have two girls at home, and the fact is that one of three teenage girls will be pregnant before eighteen. Odds on, it will be one of mine." He told me he didn't know what to do to protect them, to protect other girls like them, but now he's joined us, and he knows he can do *something*. He goes to his county commissioner and asks: Do you have any prenatal health programs? Do you have programs to educate kids about pregnancy and family? If you don't, you'd better!'
>
> Another father, a second generation Cuban-American, told me how his getting involved helped his

children. He was working as a volunteer translator for us, and one day he said to me, "My kids are proud of me!" I said, "Your kids have always been proud of you." And he said, "Yeah, but when my son found out what I was doing here, he said, 'Hey great, Dad, you're helping *me!* '" Later this same teenager asked if he could help us. He told me, "They don't let me vote, but I can do everything else. I can knock on doors, answer questions." He was *proud*.

Political fatherlove isn't only about the future; it shapes the future, but it also helps shape our kids in the present. A cautionary note: It's possible to place too much emphasis on politics, at least as we have come to think of politics. The political fatherman is an extension of the community fatherman (who is an extension of the nurturing fatherman). Focusing on the reform of public institutions without equal or surpassing emphasis on reinvigorating the grassroots community is a mistake. John McKnight writes in *Social Policy:*

Despite legions of therapists, social workers, and bureaucrats, we have created crime-making correctional systems, sickness-making health systems, and stupid-making schools.

This system is set up for failure because it excludes the most important component of society: the community, the social sphere made up of family, friends, neighbors, neighborhood associations, clubs, civic groups, local enterprises, churches, ethnic associations, temples, local unions, local government, and local media. These are the social institutions that serve as the basic context for enabling people to make their contributions.

McKnight points out correctly, that "policy makers build a world based on what each person lacks or needs—a model based on deficiency." Communities are built upon recognizing capacity: "the whole depth—weaknesses and capacities—of each member."[76] And, as writers Paul Leinberger and Bruce Tucker state:

> The possibility and hope for community lie not in some worked-up commitment or idealist revival of selected traditions but in the everyday working assumption that one is far more profoundly (and mysteriously) connected to other people than merely as one of millions of isolated actors outside time and culture. . . . But the emerging kind of community is likely to arise out of ad hoc associations and far-flung networks.[77]

Politics can play a useful role in rebuilding community and reweaving common values, but ultimately, community is personal: The father transcends mere politics when he takes his son or daughter on a nighttime walk into the neighborhood, connecting with something mysterious within the psyche and on the block; when he co-ops at his child's day care or joins a parent patrol at his son's school or takes his daughter with him on a voter registration drive.

Building the village demands risk. And this risk—this emotional reaching out—is good for fathers.

John Parr tells of how he spoke up at a community meeting on an issue that affected the future of his child's school. He is an experienced man, accustomed to speaking all over the country before large groups of people, often on controversial political topics.

"As we started organizing parents, I realized that in all my years of being a professional, working in the area of community change, I had never operated at such a personally intense level," says Parr.

He was awed by the single parents who sacrificed simply to come to the meetings. He was impressed by how the children who attended these meetings looked at their parents: with respect.

The parents asked Parr to testify, on their behalf, at a school board meeting.

"When we got to the school board meeting, there were about seventy-five parents there. I knew most of the school board members personally. I'm a pro at this kind of thing. I was sitting there waiting to testify, and Sandy (his wife) said to me, 'Are you okay?' I said, 'Why?' She said, 'You're *nervous*. You're jumping all around.' And I said to her, 'Actually, I'm terrified.' " This was, as he put it, "the first time I had ever done it as a consumer, or as a father." The hopes of the other parents were riding on his performance. "As I stood up to testify for my own child and these other children, I was shaking."

This was different from anything he had experienced as a political professional. This risk was not abstract. It was the first time in months, Parr said, that he had felt truly alive.

Sometimes life goes into slow motion, and you see things clearly. The other morning was such a moment. I saw clearly what was at stake, if we do not rebuild the village.

This was my morning to co-op at Matthew's preschool. I am beginning to love his classroom, with its flop-eared rabbit and dimwitted guinea pig. (The guinea pig sometimes comes home with us on weekends. I like to call it the Potato on Wheels. "No, Dad," Matthew says, "his name is Kris!") On this particular morning, there were two other parents co-oping, so the teacher decided that, with this much car power, we should take the dozen four-year-olds on a field trip to Ben & Jerry's Ice Cream Store.

We buckled in the kids and, in caravan, went a few blocks to the mini-mall. The teacher went inside to order cones. The parents stayed outside with the kids, arranging them at the picnic tables. It was a nice moment in the cool air.

Suddenly there was a commotion across the street. I looked up. Four or five homeless men were sprawled along the front wall of a seedy liquor store. A couple of them were holding brown bags. One was saying something in the direction of a truck, where someone sat, invisible. The truck was like a thousand other pushing, shoving pickups you see on the freeway, a small, blue, dented Japanese pickup with oversize tires. Now the door of the pickup opened, and a young man with long, stringy hair, wearing a muscle shirt and heavy boots, stepped out quickly and approached the men. They exchanged more words.

This was where time began to slow down.

The young man returned to the pickup, reached inside. He walked back toward the homeless men, and his arm moved up in a long, slow arc. He was holding a handgun, so heavy that the muscles of his arm bulged. His face was purple with rage, and approaching the men, he swung the gun back and forth in front of their faces.

The homeless men fell silent and sat still. The moment seemed frozen in the air.

This is like television, I thought, and then realized that I was with a dozen children who, sitting low, did not know what was happening.

"Kids, listen to me . . ." I said. I knew I should tell them to get down. . . .

Then the man turned again, still in a rage, swaggered back to his truck, and sat there, invisible again.

One of my fellow parents, a mother, came to attention quicker than I did. Very calmly, she said, "Kids, let's go inside."

We quickly shepherded them in.

We got them to the back of the ice-cream parlor, and then I went back to watch the street. The pickup was still there. I couldn't make out the muddied license plate number. After a while, the pickup pulled out and sped away.

"That does it, I'm moving back to Canada, where they have gun control," said the teacher, shaken, but trying to be light.

I said that I think about moving, too. But where?

The kids had not seen what had happened, and we did not tell them.

Later, as we drove away, I saw several police cars pull up in front of the liquor store; the officers were roughly searching the homeless men. Perhaps a witness had reported that someone was waving a gun, and perhaps the cops assumed that one of the homeless men was the culprit.

Then they faded in the rear-view mirror.

I felt I should have done something more. But what? Walk across the street and get the license plate number? Nope. With the kids there, we could not risk a confrontation. Tell the cops the homeless men weren't guilty? It was too late, or so it seemed at the time.

The moment drifted by, like a slow river. And I began to feel the growing, dull anger that so many of us as parents suppress most of our days.

Danger isn't exactly the issue. All of us are in some kind of danger every moment of our lives. Driving is dangerous.

FatherLove

But physical danger aside, this exposure, this threat, does something to us.

The exposure is invasive, assaultive, violating. It discolors our days. It infects us with a kind of rage that can take on a life of its own.

Two things are certain. Life is becoming a lot more like television. And our rage must be directed toward rebuilding our communities.

VI

Finding Our Place in Time

SEVERAL YEARS AGO, ON FATHER'S DAY, I DROVE MY TWO
boys, then ages two and eight, to a nearby lake. We spent
the afternoon walking along the bank; they ran ahead, in
their life jackets, sometimes fishing—the younger boy with
a lead weight on a line tied to the tip of a two-foot rod—
more often digging along the bank for bugs or throwing
rocks in the water.

Well, fishing isn't about catching fish anyway.

I was using a new fly rod. I do not know much about
fly fishing, but I had discovered the sense of connectedness
that fly fishing gives, unlike more typical rituals of high-
powered bass fishing, which has, as a culture, become so
high-tech, competitive, and loud that it virtually destroys
any sense of connection to nature, or to time. Because of
this new interest, I had dug through the utility room and
found a corroded tin canister. On the bank, I opened the
canister, which was, for me, a kind of time capsule.

FatherLove

It was filled with large, old flies and hand-painted poppers. They had once been used by someone else for northern pike or, perhaps, for bass. I carefully removed one of the flies from its fastening and tied it to my line. It looked like a frog, with feathers that trailed out behind it.

In the mid-1960s, in Kansas, my best friend Pete and I would often walk over to Red Hoth's house. Red, who was in his sixties, had suffered a stroke in 1952 while fishing, and he was paralyzed from the neck down, except for one arm. Pete visited Red because of compassion; I went for the fishing stories. And I went because, like many kids, I was looking for a father figure.

Red would spin his stories out so vividly that it seemed almost as if we were on some North Woods lake long ago with the early morning mist rising around the boat, his bed.

On one of our last visits, we arrived to find a large tackle box and a set of bamboo fly rods at the foot of Red's bed. He gave all of his old gear, which he loved, to us.

Years passed away. So did Red. Piece by piece, most of this equipment somehow disappeared, except this last tin canister and its contents, which had not been used in nearly forty years.

So now, I flipped the fly into the water to show my older son, and we watched the feathers transform into kicking legs as it moved through the water. I told my son about Red. It's the small stories that count most, I think. Then I pulled the rod up and made a long, rare, perfect cast, and the frog moved out across the smooth water in a gradual arc, and it fell through time.

Finding one's place in generational time—the fourth dimension of fatherhood—is part of the expression and experience of fatherlove. Mothers, connected by the umbilical cord to past and future, are blessed with more frequent biological reminders of the natural cycles and rhythms of time, nature, and the generations. But as a man moves deeper into his fatherhood, he travels beyond his physical home and village, into time and the spirit.

Old distinctions between generations are blurring; no matter what our age, we wear Reeboks and address each other by first names. Liberation from age stereotypes is a good thing. But we suffer a kind of time poverty, not only because we do not have enough dreamtime, but because time itself seems to have lost its story line. Without a sense of generativity, we feel disconnected, lost in time.

In psychoanalyst Erik Erikson's theory of personality growth, the seventh of eight stages of growth is generativity versus self-absorption. The essence of generativity is involvement in the development and well-being of the next generation. In order to avoid stagnation and enter the final stage of adult development—integrity—adults must be concerned and contributing to the next generation. Doing this, we can achieve a sense of integrity and satisfaction with our own life cycle and its place in time

In this dimension, a father finds meaning in relationships, actions, and values—as opposed to the sense of despair he is likely to feel when it is too late to try again. To avoid this despair, to find that fulfillment, each moment with your children must be treasured as part of a line that connects the past with the future. Alfred Korzybski, a pioneer in the field of semantics, who identified human beings as "time-binding" creatures, wrote: "We alone are able to transcend time, to bind the past, present and future together with words." We do this, in part, through the stories we tell.

Story-telling is an old, nearly forgotten art. Lynne

Cheney, former chairperson of the National Endowment for the Humanities, describes the emergence of a Southwestern Native American art form from the Pueblo tradition that is an outgrowth of storytelling. The originator of this art form, in the early 1960s, was a potter from the Cochiti Pueblo in New Mexico, who thought of her grandfather telling stories as she shaped clay into scenes in which figurines of listeners, often children, were gathered around a storyteller. "No background knowledge is required to look into the faces of the storytellers and see something that is at once mysterious and familiar," according to Cheney. "Their mouths are often open, often in a stylized *O*. Their eyes are shut or gazing fixedly upward as they perform an amazing feat that we all take for granted: creating other worlds in this one; vivifying times that have passed, people that are gone forever, events that are known only through memory."

The Pueblo artists who create the storytellers say that these figures represent an older way of life, before television, before we began to run faster than time.

One way to find our place in time is to expose children to more history and to the great books—not simply as required texts, but as stories that offer moral and spiritual guidance, that connect us to accumulated wisdom and experience, and to our own fathers. More important, we have the opportunity to tell our children, and potentially our grandchildren, stories of their past and stories of the future.

Ultimately, for fathers, the art of storytelling—of describing our place in time—is a way of life. It's not just in books; it's personal.

When I would ask parents to describe their feelings about this fourth dimension, they at first said that they have not thought much about it, but slowly some of them began to tell stories.

Women often spoke about their husbands' sensitivity to time. During a discussion about fatherhood, one mother, Margaret Garber, who is a historian, spoke about how she and her husband sometimes talk about time. "Imagine that you are holding hands with your grandfather, and your grandfather is holding hands with his grandfather. Suddenly you're back to the Civil War. Then you have a couple more hand-holdings, and you're back in medieval times. It's not that long. If you think of how those people were raised and how they in turn raised their grandchildren, you feel so connected with time. It works both ways. I imagine myself holding my granddaughter's hand, and she is holding her grandchild's hand."

"My husband and I just went away last weekend for a few days by ourselves, up in the mountains," said Katherine Hopkins-Cordua, in a San Diego group. On the long drive, they began to talk about the years to come, and her husband asked her, "Do you think about the future and what happens to the children? Where do you think they'll be in twenty-five years?"

Katherine said she doesn't think about it but that her husband does:

He is an artist, and he gets off on these flights of fantasy. He will fantasize about where one of the children might be in thirty years. He often does this driving in the car. He was telling me about these visions that he has, thirty, forty, one hundred years into the future, of our children and their children and even beyond. And *I* think concretely, in terms of school starting in a few weeks and maybe planning for a vacation in November. As I put my measly little bit of money into their college funds, in a nebulous sort of way I think about the future, but he'll have these emotional flights of fancy about the children, and I won't.

I think he sees himself in the future as kind of a benevolent, wise mentor for them. And I think he will be, because he's very intuitive. He'll say, 'If Caitlin goes to Harvard, I think she'll go and write her dissertation right outside of Walden Pond. Then she'll go to England, do a fellowship. And Elaine will go to plumbing school, learn a trade, and make more money than the rest of us; but she'll create a foundation and they'll finally cure AIDS. And Caitlin and Elaine's children will . . ."

My husband weaves this web about the future. It makes our car trips much shorter.

Dick Thompson, a Presbyterian pastor and father, who is in his forties, told a story about his father, a retired music teacher, who taught for thirty-five years in the same junior high:

Because my dad was a teacher, he had summers off. So my brother and I had Dad all summer long. What a rare thing. We'd take long vacations with him and my mom, traveling from Los Angeles to Iowa to see relatives. We'd take comic books, and my dad would make my brother and me slingshots, and he'd make scooters out of roller skates and boards, which is actually death on wheels; you hit a crack and you're meat.

On the long trips in the backseat, my dad would sense that we were going out of our minds, and he would stop the car, and he'd line up tin cans on a log, and we'd throw rocks at them, and my mom would sit and watch us throw rocks for twenty minutes. Today, I think those images still operate within me. They still inform me about being a man and a father.

Dick laughs with pleasure at the memory and then tells a story about a flute.

> My dad went through high school playing a flute. He was so good he got a scholarship to college because of it. World War Two hit, and he became part of the army marching band. In North Africa he was captured by some of Rommel's panzers. He had to bury his Browning automatic so the Germans wouldn't get it. He was in a German prison for two years. The Red Cross shipped band instruments in to help the prisoners' morale. My dad picked out a silver Selmer flute and played it in lots of productions in the camp. . . .
>
> At the end of the war, the Germans force-marched the prisoners west, away from the Russians. A lot of the instruments were too bulky to pack, but a flute is small, and my father was able to put it into his pack and cross the Elbe River. He brought it home.
>
> That flute was the same one he used to teach with for thirty-five years. I grew up watching him organize stage bands, assemblies, and I am filled with the images of my dad conducting. I have images of this flute all through my life, even before I was born. I never took up the flute myself, but today, my nine-year-old daughter Julia owns my father's flute.
>
> In December, 1991, Julia had her very first recital. My dad came down from L.A., and Julia and my dad played flute duets. As I watched them, I became aware of something. Here's my dad on the left of the stage, and Julia is on the right. I'm crouched down with the video camera, and I'm panning back and forth, and

suddenly I realized the power of being in between. There was a continuity there, and the flute was the continuity of the generations.

Not all of us are so well connected in time. If we wish to find our place in time, for our own sake and the sake of our children, those of us with traumatic memories of our fathers struggle to mend the long line that stretches from the past to the future. Making a settlement with our own fathers—or with our memories of them, with their stories—is necessary before we can pass these stories on to our children and form new stories of our own. Many men "harbor a profound wish for a perfect father who really will save them from the risks and anxieties of making a marriage work, raising children and dealing with success and failure in the world of work," writes Samuel Osherson, author of *Finding Our Fathers*. He continues:

> An Odysseus brought down from the clouds by the gods rather than ol' Dad who let you down and leaves you to deal with life on your own. Healing the wounded father means accepting some of our aloneness, giving up the wish that Dad'll take care of us. There is grief in that loss of the fantasies of the all-powerful father we wish we had. Accepting that loss means tolerating the wish for such a father and seeing that it is really a childhood dream.[78]

Osherson suggests that healing the wounds left by our fathers involves a long process of grieving and that this may be part of "the normal developmental process of mourning that has been identified as characteristic of mid-life." He has been impressed, he writes, by how many men cry when they come to realize what they have not gotten from their fathers. "In trying to understand our fathers, we confront the depths of our neediness and that of our fathers."[79]

Again and again, in my interviews with fathers, they said that the primary shaper of their fathering was the determination not to repeat their fathers' mistakes. If their fathers had been absent, they determined to be present; if their fathers had beaten them, they determined to be gentle; if their fathers had been emotionally detached, they determined to hold and kiss their children. Sometimes, they said, they heard their fathers' voices in their own mouths, and this scared them. Sometimes they heard their fathers' good words in their heart, and this pleased them. Sometimes they assaulted their fathers, living or dead, with strange weapons.

One man, who is in his forties, described his father as cold and distant:

> My Little League coach died a couple years ago from a blood disorder. When he died, I cried. I remembered how he gave me the strokes that I needed, growing up. He used to take me down to the YMCA on Friday nights. He used to care for me. My dad just never had the time to do that. He was detached. To this day, he's not much on close contact. So now when I see him, I grab him and kiss him on the lips. I do it jokingly. I know it makes him uncomfortable.

This man laughed as he told of kissing his father. I wondered how his rage at his own father, and his unforgiveness of him, affects his relationship with his own children.

Osherson suggests that one way of healing what he calls "the wounded father within you" is to plunge into your father's history, to find ways to empathize with your father's pain. "The women's movement has furnished many daughters a way of understanding and forgiving their mothers, but men have little corresponding sense of their fathers. We have to understand our fathers' struggles."

Osherson suggests that for many men this process of exploring their fathers' lives and pain gets blocked by disinterest or fear, and some prefer to avoid reconciliation and to keep the connection broken. "It's striking in therapy to ask bitter patients, 'Would you take love from your father now, if he were to give it?' A startling number will reply, 'No!'" But it is still possible for a man "to engage an absent father in a dialogue of emotional growth. The son may write down imaginary dialogues between himself and his father and other family members, or write unmailed letters to a dead or absent father." He may also record his father's stories. For some men, these stories can replace the anger and disappointment with acceptance and understanding. Osherson writes:

Ultimately it is the internal image of their fathers that all men must heal. This process involves not just exploring the past, but also the present and future—ways of being male that reflect a richer, fuller sense of self than the narrow images that dominated the past. . . . Becoming a parent is clearly a part of reworking an identification with the father. . . . At bottom, healing the wounded father is a process of untangling the myths and fantasies sons learn growing up about self, mother and father, and which we act out every day with bosses and wives and children. It means constructing a satisfying sense of manhood both from our opportunities in a time of changing sex-roles and by "diving into the wreck" of the past and retrieving a firm, sturdy appreciation of the heroism and failure in our fathers' lives.[80]

One father, Tom Katsis, sitting with a men's group at a church in San Diego, spoke movingly of a reconciliation he had with his father, after his father's death. "My dad wasn't very present when I was young. In the thirty-two years—certainly in the first twenty years—of my life, I don't ever remember our whole family sitting around and having a dinner. It was a very fragmented family. So when I was going through my divorce, I was terrified that I would become like my father, cut off from my kids, like he was.

"My father died when I was thirty-two. During a two- or three-year period before he died, he started to reach out to me. I was living and teaching in Sioux City, Iowa, which is my hometown. My dad would call me up and say things like, 'Tom, are you going to go golfing?' I'd say, 'I might go golfing.'

"And my dad would say, 'If you go, let me go along, I just want to ride along.'

"But I was so into parenting my own children, and still probably mad at the fact that he had never really been there for me when I was a child, that I avoided him."

Looking back, Tom wishes that he had picked up on his dad's signals.

Now he thinks often of his father's life. "My dad never had a car. He was born in Greece, came to the United States when he was seven years old. He was a shoe repairman, like my grandfather was a shoe repairman before him. So my dad always took the bus to his shoe shop and came home at night.

"I wasn't very proud of my dad. From the ages of nine to fourteen I lived with an aunt because my family was so

184

fragmented. My dad was drinking and gambling. I was only about a mile away from the house, but there was this real distant feeling. I remember getting on the bus in downtown Sioux City one night to go home after working at this restaurant where I worked. I was about fourteen. And I'm way at the back of the bus, and my dad got on the front of the bus, and I hid. I was ashamed because he was always coming home after having been drinking, and he was really convivial and really friendly with everybody, but it was that false kind of friendliness because if you've been drinking a lot, you're everybody's friend. . . ."

Tom stopped talking for a while and looked away. The other men in the group were silent.

"A couple of years ago, I wrote a letter to him and took it back to Sioux City and read it over his grave and burned the letter over his grave. I finally wanted to grieve the loss of the fact that I did not have a father who was close to me when I was little.

"I was mad as hell, and I wanted to get rid of that. Once I did, I was able to forgive my dad and accept that he was who he was and was doing the best he could, and now I am doing the best I can as a father."

Samuel Osherson has eloquently described the process of healing the past, but I've come to consider part of this fourth dimension as a confrontation, in the present, with future grief.

Tom, sitting in the church basement with the other men continued to speak. "When I got divorced, my kids were ten and nine. I was really in a panicky state. I thought, what's going to happen if I don't keep up with my relationship with my children? So we used to have a lot of talks about abandonment. Two weeks after I separated I was with them one night, and I said, "Do you feel afraid of what's happening?"

The told their father that they did.

And Tom told them, "From now until the day I die, if you're afraid of something, or if something's not happening the way you want it to happen, tell me about it. I may not have the answer, and I may not satisfy you with the answer I come up with, but I want you to tell me what scares you."

His kids are now twenty-six and twenty-five.

"I want to be there. If, in their late twenties, early thirties, early forties, they go through a crisis, a divorce, a bad sickness or injury, I want to be there. And I don't want them to stop loving me. Until my son was sixteen, we had a thing called the super-hug. He would jump into my arms and wrap his legs around me, and he'd be like a monkey clinging to me. He's big now; he's six-foot-one. Recently, he wanted me to be the super *hugee*. I took this running jump at him, I jumped up, he grabbed me, and I wrapped my legs around him. We reversed the super-hug.

"If I live to be 90, *I want to be a dad all the way until I die.*"

That sentence touched me. Perhaps, as fathers, we carry with us a certain amount of pre-grief, as it were, for the day when our children will leave home. I know that this is true in my case, or at least, at that moment, I realized it. Could it be that this grieving for the future is one of the reasons that fathers tend to distance themselves from their children, that adds to the fear of being too invested? Do mothers feel this grief in quite this same way? Perhaps they may feel it more about their daughters than their sons, since it is part of the development of a daughter to push her mother away, just as it is part of the plan for sons to push their fathers away for a long while.

FatherLove

A couple of years ago, when my son Jason and I went to a baseball game, the car steamed over, and we ended up waiting for the traffic to dissipate. I did not want to get stuck in the line again and have the engine overheat, so we sat in the dark in the car for over an hour.

As we sat there, a carload of teenage boys went by, the boys hooting and squawking and waving various limbs from the windows.

"Why do teenagers dress so funny and act so stupid?" asked Jason suddenly. He was nine then.

I thought about this for a while. "Because they're separating from their parents," I finally said. "They want to be different from their parents."

Jason was silent for a while. I glanced over. I could not see his face in the dark, only his silhouette in the light of passing cars.

Then he said, with a worried tone in his voice, "I don't want to separate. I love you and Mom."

He had interpreted what I had said literally. As we talked more, I realized that the only way he had probably heard that verb used—to separate—was in the context of marriage and divorce.

I explained as best I could that I had meant that teenagers must become their own people but that they do not have to split entirely from their parents. As I spoke, I realized I was trying to convince myself of this as much as explain it to him. He seemed satisfied, and we sat there in the dark some more. It was a good moment, and we felt very close.

A few months later, my wife experienced a similar moment with our then five-year-old son. Matthew was sitting in a rocking chair across the room from my wife. He was sitting quietly, holding Blue Bear, his favorite stuffed animal. He looked at his mother, and suddenly his face fell, and he said, "Mom, I miss being a baby. . . ." He dissolved in tears, and his mother held him.

He had suddenly remembered his bottle, and he had missed it. In a flash of awareness, he had realized his place in time, and that time is moving.

Now, sitting with these fathers, I realized intensely that, like Tom, I wish to be a father to Matthew and Jason until the day I die and that my fathering is not limited by time and, perhaps, not even by death. This is a comforting thought, and it also makes parenting seem a far more permanent and important thing than this notion, which our culture sometimes seems to endorse of temporary caretaking.

Howard Hurst, a member of this group, is in his seventies. White-haired, gentle, he is a former farmer and military man, and a grandfather. I mentioned that this idea of being a father until the day you die leads to another point, which is that perhaps one of the rewards of being a good father is that you may get to become a good grandfather. A grandfatherman. And I wonder if this idea is clear to men in our culture.

"I think it's clear to some men, but not to most," he said. Then he told part of his own story:

My father died when I was twelve. He had been a farmer and a truck driver, and he died in an automobile accident. I felt deprived by his absence. My mother did not remarry. I had two brothers and a sister; I was the second child. This was in the 1930s. Life was tough in those days. You had to go out and make a living, make an income of some kind and bring it all home, throw it in a pot. My grandfather lived not too far from us, so we saw him frequently. My grandfather became sort of a father to me. He was a great guy.

Hardworking; he was a farmer too. Worked hard all his life, and he was full of peace and happiness. He thought that everybody was good. Sometimes I would work outside with him on the farm. And then he would always spend his evenings in a nice lawn chair. After dinner we'd sit back there, and he'd tell me stories. Experience stories, mostly.

I was always a little bit unhappy with my father because he died. I didn't really understand it until several weeks ago when we were talking in this group. I missed my father, I missed him very much. It finally got through to me at this last meeting that I had been angry at my father all these years for dying, for getting killed. That's hard to live with. He was a good man; he had a lot of love. It was time to get on with my own life.

Howard, whose voice was very gentle, said that his grandfather may not have been a real father, but he did pass on to Howard a good working definition of manhood.

Being a good man is being able to take hold and do the hard work. To make decisions, as decisions are needed to be made, and to make them honest. He taught me one very important thing: you are responsible for your own decisions. Every step of the way. If you make a decision to fall on your face, that's your responsibility. If you make a decision to stand up straight and walk straightforward, that's your responsibility, and keep going. Also, my grandfather tried to instill in me a strong sense of what is right and what is wrong, and to be kind and generous. Don't turn away everybody who has done wrong. And don't hang on to everybody that's done right. Grab on to both of them and try to see good things in each. This is something that I try to carry on to my kids. I'm trying to teach my grandson that now. He's just six.

You have to start conditioning yourself early in the program. Early in your adult life, you have to condition yourself to the fact that as your kids grow up, there is going to be some separation, that you're sort of like an accordian, you'll have to stretch and expand and contract as they need you and don't need you as much. The key thing for you to keep in mind is that they must know at all times that you love them. L O V E. And you have to tell them that, you can't let them assume that. You have to tell them that you love them.

You also have to let them know that as time goes on, they're going to have to experiment a little bit further, get their feet a little bit more wet. Go out and stretch their arms and their legs and their mind. But at the same time, you need to say to them, 'When you get to the point where you need some help, I'm here. I'll always be here to help you. To this day, when they call me, sometimes they say; 'I'm so glad you said that and that you were there.' There's a real payoff to being a father, as time goes by.

Ken, a man in his thirties, a lawyer, had listened to this conversation without speaking. He appeared increasingly uncomfortable. Now he spoke up:

"I *don't* want to be a father the rest of my life. I mean, I'm stuck with it." He laughed. "Let me clarify that. I *will* be a father for the rest of my life. But I don't think I want to be a *daddy* for the rest of my life. By daddy I mean the father that's there during the growing-up years. I think I'm going to be a father to my sons for the rest of their lives, but it changes—it's hard for me to articulate. Just as Howard's father is still there. . . ."

He turned and spoke to Howard:

Even though your father physically died when you were twelve, your father is still there, somehow. I *am becoming right now* the father that I will be for the rest of my son's life. It's these next fifteen years that will be my fatherhood to him. Certainly, after he grows up, whether he grows up at eighteen or grows up at thirty, after he grows up I'll still be around, hopefully, and still be there for what I can offer at that time. But the daddy that I will be imparting to him is being done now.

Howard, I'm at the front end of the process that you have completed. At least in my mind, you have completed it. And you can see it as a continuing process. But I am much younger than you. My challenge is to make it happen now. I feel great pressure in the sense that there's no making it up. That anything that I do or don't do in the next fifteen years is not going to be solved when my son is thirty-five. I've got a certain number of years to get it all in, and then the boy is going to grow up and has got to have the tools to go on with it. I can't always be there: I might die. I might fall on times when I can't help him, so I've got to give him that stuff, whatever that "father stuff" is, I've got to give it now.

I'll always be Ken. But the father my children take with them, when they get up in the morning and drive to work, come home and become fathers, will be the daddy I am now. That daddy will be inside of my sons.

To me, this conversation revealed a paradoxical truth: that we have our whole lives, if we live and if our sons live to be fathers, and that is part of the joy and the payoff of fathering; but fathers must also face the uncomfortable truth that they have only a short time in which to be their children's psychological father, the *remembrance* father that Ken described.

Steve Garber, the poet/plumber/father, and husband of Margaret, described the paradox of time and parenting. "We spend a lot of time as parents talking about the future or the past, and we don't deal with the present, but our children are watching us right now."

And, he said, in that moment, the future *and* the past are forming.

I remember one particular moment when I was putting my sons to bed, the youngest on the lower bunk, the oldest on the upper. I had recently set up clip-on reading lamps in each of their bunks, and they had been very appreciative of this.

As I installed the lamps, I mentioned to both boys, "You could hang blankets around the bunk here and make a fort, and you'd have your little light on inside." Yeah! they had said. A few nights later, tucking the boys in, I looked up at Jason and at his bunk and the light and said, "You know, Jason, you're close to the ceiling there. The next time we get some big pieces of cardboard, maybe you could put up cardboard walls around your bunk. . . ." And he looked at me with love and understanding, a look that said, *I'm almost eleven and may be getting too old for that, but Dad wants me to play for him.* It was a fine moment, perhaps one of those he will remember in time.

New York's nonprofit Manpower Demonstration Research Corporation, which funds counseling programs in eleven cities, asks fathers to write obituaries for themselves in the voices of their children, as if their children were writing them. I wonder: What would my obituary say, if Jason or Matthew were to write it? What would your children write?

Mentoring a younger man is another paternal link in time. Pete, a man who has, over the years, been my mentor and sometimes surrogate father, is now in his sixties. One day, while we talked, he began to wonder aloud what a man must think about at the end, as he lay in a hospital bed, perhaps pulled inward until no muscle could move, when nurses whispered, when the world moved on without him. What would he think of? As the sensations of the present passed, he thought that perhaps his children would come into sharper focus. Even now, Pete's memories of his children seem sharper, more crystalline.

He is not a particularly introspective man. But sitting in his office, now, he leans back and says he never really missed having a father. His father left when he was a small child. Years later, as an adult, he met his father, but the man was a zero, a cypher, who had nothing of interest to say. There was no link to the past at all; no link to the future either. "I wish he had never come. It was useless."

He is not particularly bitter about this, simply puzzled that this man who was his father would have no memories of his own child. But Pete will have memories. He is a good father, and he somehow knew how to love his children as children, to respect them, to offer fatherlove to other young women and men who needed it.

As he talks now of his children, his eyes shine, and he laughs and launches into story after story about his grown boys, all now successful and strong in different ways. None of these stories is very long; all are the descriptions of moments. This is what he will have, and he shows no fear.

Listening to him, I wonder what dreaming memories will come to me. Unlike Pete, I do fear that end. I wonder if the memories of my own father will somehow overshadow the memories of my own boys. Will these moments with my children be strong enough, potent enough, sharp and loving enough, to bury ones from my own childhood? This is not a comfortable question for some of us, but it's a good question. What moments are we making, now, and how will these moments strengthen and calm and caress us so much later, when the nurses murmur?

"I can do it, Dad."

That's the sentence that you wait to hear, I guess, the one that says the boy is growing, starting to separate, and it makes you proud and a little sad.

"I can tie the knot," Jason said as I handed him a lure. I showed him how but kept part of the information in reserve. For later, I said, when the boat isn't in these waves, but I knew that the real reason was the sadness.

Matthew turned around from his station in the bow and grinned. The sun flashed from his glasses.

A few moments passed. "Would you like to drive the boat?" I asked Jason.

"Sure!" he said. He was wearing his cumbersome child's life jacket, which he detests. He balanced his body low in the boat. All arms and legs, he moved back to sit next to me and took the handle of the engine. He was practicing and succeeding. I was practicing, too, trying to stifle my habitual irritation, trying not to insist that the fishing be perfect, trying to let the boys be boys.

FatherLove

It had been nearly a year since we last fished on this lake. The handle then had vibrated hard in Jason's hand. He had been near tears with frustration. At that age, turning the handle to the right in order to turn the boat left was a difficult abstraction to understand.

Now he knows more about paradox.

He sat up straight. I could sense the new strength he felt in his back and arm. The boat pointed true. He was smiling, hair pushed back by the wind.

In my family, fishing has always been more than fishing. Sometimes I feel that I am connected to the past and the future by monofilament line.

A few weeks earlier, my brother and I had flown my mother's body back to Missouri. We had returned to the lake where we grew up, and we went fishing in her honor. My brother joked that he wished that we had brought her to the lake instead of leaving her at the cemetery. He said we could have propped her up and put a rod in her hand. He said this with love and longing.

My rod pulled down. "Cut the engine," I told Jason. He searched for the button. The trout flashed orange. I reached down and hit the button. Jason stood up. "Pull your line in!" I said.

I took a breath. I like to tell people that fishing is not about fishing and that I don't really care if I catch them. The first part is true, the second part is a lie. My father was a sullen fisherman. My mother was incandescent. When my mother lost a fish, the hills were alive with the sounds of cannonballs and missiles, bursts of the artfully profane.

As I wrestled the fish, I accidentally whacked Jason with my elbow. I swore, and we both laughed. Matthew was looking on the wrong side of the boat. "What fish?" he said.

I brought it in, unhooked it, and held it in my hands. Matthew inspected it closely. These days, I usually release fish. To hook and hurt a fish and then to let it go to save it is morally grayer than killing for food, but so it is with paradox.

I stroked its belly and let it go. Stunned, it slowly turned in the water, on its side. "That's not exactly what I had in mind," I said. I reached out for it. "I should have run water through its gills." Just then, it awoke and dived.

We moved down the lake. A year ago, my older son was bored with fishing. Now he had turned serious and was casting accurately with long, smooth arcs.

The sun was low. In a cove at the end of the lake, we got out of the boat and walked through tall grass to where the creek widened into a sandy pool before entering the deep water. Newly hatched tadpoles swam in the pool, and a frog hugged the bottom.

The older boy was suddenly in the water, chasing the frog.

The air was cool and soothing. I looked out across the lake and then back at the pool. In an instant, the younger boy had stripped completely, except for his glasses. He was standing in the creek in water up to his crotch. He let loose a stream of his own and held his hands high and screeched with joy. As the earth turned, I watched my sons, and I was amazed at their beauty.

VII

The Spiritual Life of Fathers

A FEW YEARS AGO, I EXPERIENCED ONE FATHER'S CONNECTION to his fatherhood and nature and the world beyond. This memory is in Arizona, at dawn. . . .

This is the time of day that Navajos call "grandfather talking god." When the strip of white light rises over the mountains, there is no evil, no pain; the dust of the previous day has settled.

In this white dawn, Steve Darden, a thirty-one-year-old Navajo, and an important man in Flagstaff, Arizona, drove his Ford Ranger on the dirt road up the side of the San Francisco Peaks, the remains of an extinct volcano. To the Navajos, the mountain is "grandmother," one of four holy mountains.

The first Navajo to be elected to the Flagstaff City Council, Darden had agreed to show me the mountain, but on his own terms. "I will not go up just for you," he had said several times. "I go up for my own purposes."

An elk was standing on the gravel road ahead of us, and Darden stopped the truck. "If it crosses the road," he said, "we'll have to turn back."

After a moment of indecision, the elk returned the way it had come, running down through the firs and birches, haunches moving in jerky, slow motion. It joined five others, blended into the brush. They watched us. Darden breathed quietly. He pushed his fingers into a tiny deerskin pouch. "I was wondering last night what I would see; would I meet a coyote, a trickster, who knows how to manipulate? I would have turned back; but the *dzeh*, the elk, is a good sign."

From the pouch he took corn pollen and sprinkled it out the window, and eyes shut, head down, he spoke a Navajo prayer. And then he told how, a long time ago, the Holy People had punished the *Dine*, the Navajos, because man had abused animals, and man was separated from them. "When we enter their territory now, we must pray, we must go through a transflux, a transition so that we can be among them."

He started the engine, and we began again to climb the mountain.

The dawn moon was up over a long field grazed by cattle with plastic clips in their ears. Darden parked the truck, and we walked under a ski lift. We crossed the field and went up into the trees. "We call the mountain grandmother because her hair is white," he said. We passed through white aspens with trunks carved with graffiti. "This is where I get angry. Beer bottles, drugs, all disharmony. It's like slobbering on your grandmother."

For a quarter mile, he said nothing. He moved quickly, listening, watching the ground, pausing to watch a deer move off into the pines. He stopped next to a spruce seedling.

FatherLove

Four times a year he makes these pilgrimages; this time he had come to give thanks for his new son, who had been born a few days earlier. He came to give thanks for his election to the city council. And to ask for guidance.

He knelt in the leaves and needles, bending over until his forehead almost touched the ground. His *chongo*, the bun of long hair tied with cloth, was white in the dim light. He began to speak in Navajo, his voice rising and falling. The wind moved the trees. He dug little holes in the ground and from his pockets took campaign fliers and buttons, pieces of turquoise and coral. He planted these artifacts in the mountain, returning them to their maker.

After a long while, he stood up. "I want my boy to have a strong back, a straight life, like this little spruce. A lot of things around this evergreen have fallen; the tree that you are sitting on fell a long time ago. And yet new, straight life always comes along."

On the way back down the mountain, he stopped the truck and pointed with excitement. There, on the opposite side of the road from where they had been, were six bull elk. They were standing much closer now, heads raised with wide, velvety antlers.

"In eight years," he said, "I have only seen elk on the mountain twice. This is a good day."

He said he was thinking of his son.

And I thought of mine.

When fathers talk of fatherhood, they sometimes talk of a spiritual connection, one that is not necessarily religious but that provides them with invisible help. When they talk about this, the talk comes slowly, as if an appropriate language does not exist or has not been found or remembered. But with prompting, they talk.

One father described the fifth dimension of fatherlove, spirituality, this way:

> You can't do this alone. You can't get approval or encouragement from the child because that's the object of your activity. If you don't have a wife, or there's no communication there, and there's nobody else, maybe you turn to this inner feeling in your heart, or wherever. That's the spiritual part of fathering. You need your encouragement and approval from somewhere.

Another man, whose father had deserted him when he was an infant, described how he has filled the void left by the absent father, with God the Father, to whom he turns for guidance.

Now, personally, it doesn't matter much to me if God is a man or a woman or a politically correct cross-dresser. But I do recognize, as a father, that there is something within me or without me, something that does, on occasion, guide my parenting.

Wondering about this, I convened a discussion in my living room of clerics, rabbis, and Muslim religious leaders from around my city. Except for the Jesuit priest, all these men had children of their own.

Surely they had thoughts about the spiritual life of fathers.

Rabbi Jay Miller began: "I'm raising my children with the hope, not that they'll emulate me as a man or my wife as a woman but that they're involved in a religious community." He spoke of the bar mitzvah and bat mitzvah ceremonies (which mean "son of" or "daughter of" the community).

Why, I wondered, during a conversation about spirituality, did the word community come up so soon? "Because the home has become more of a 'small h' home," explained Eddy Samaniego, the Jesuit.

As a culture we focus too much on the isolated family, the individual parent, and not enough on what he called the "Home with a capital H." The neighborhood, the world, the universe. The priest described that, in his studies of Native American cultures, he had learned how fathers took their sons out to the world, to the woods, to introduce them to the "house beyond the tepee."

Listening to Samaniego, I thought of an experience with my firstborn last year. We were taking a family drive to Laguna Mountain, near San Diego, and stopped at a desert viewpoint. My wife and younger son stayed behind, and I took Jason down a path to a place I knew about. We walked to the very edge of the cliff—or rather, I led him to the edge. I held his arm as we sat down; then I let his arm go. We dangled our feet over the edge. We could see, far below, two ravens picking their way up a ravine. We watched shadows move out across the desert. I could feel Jason's tension ease.

The common assumption is that men are more likely than women to introduce their children to risk, that a man's spirit tends to be more adventurous than a woman's. Judging by the comparative bravery displayed by men and women within the corporate world, I am not sure this is true. My wife is physically rougher than I am when she plays with the kids. But I knew intuitively that this moment at the cliff was important, that my job as a father included taking my son to the edge of the world.

"The father is the vision maker, the connection to past

and future," said Imad Al Bahri, who is active in my city's Islamic community.

Like Al Bahri, Rabbi Martin Levin of Congregation Beth-El views the father as the keeper and transmitter of history:

As a Jew, it is important to me to transmit to my children their identity through our history. My wife will talk with them about grandparents and their aunts and uncles; I'll talk to them about their ancestors. My wife will talk with them about when they grow up and have children, and I'll talk with them about three generations from now.

This is where my life crosses the boundaries of both spirituality and religiosity, because my role as a father is attached to a sense of eternity. I am not just a person who's going to live a human life span, but I'm a link in a very long and hopefully eternal chain. In the Jewish tradition, religious identity is transmitted through the mother, but tribal identity is transmitted through the father.

We are Levites, we are the tribe of Levi. My ancestry goes back to the third son of Jacob, head of the tribe of Levi, during the time that the Jews had full independence. They were the people who ministered at the temple in Jerusalem, some were the priests involved in sacrificial worship; they were the singers and the musicians; they were not landowners. I transmit that to my children, to give them a sense of their identity. I borrow from my religious tradition, to use techniques to transmit identity and values with sacred American texts. A mother or a father can do this, but somewhere in my gut I feel that there's something masculine about it.

FatherLove

Rev. Dick Thompson, of Rancho Bernardo Community Presbyterian Church, agreed with Levin about the importance of transmitting a spiritual tradition. "For me, spirituality is my sense of where my feet are, a sense of my location in the grand scheme, my feeling that I am centered both within myself and the world, and most importantly, with God. My experience is that men tend to feel disconnected, separated."

He bases this opinion on the memorial services he has conducted for fathers—where he sits with the family to prepare the remarks and eulogy, asking them to tell him about the father, his hobbies, favorite books, art, philosophy of life, favorite passages of scripture. "I am sometimes very disappointed to see the blank looks, the shrugging shoulders, the looks across the circle to Mom, or anyone, for some answers." In his work with men, and men as fathers, Thompson believes it is important for a man to discover his own story and then to locate himself within a larger Story.

He feels sadness for the children, grown or young, that they have so little sense of continuity, personal history. It strikes him that father-absence itself may be part of the experience of spiritual uprootedness, of disconnection, of floating in time and space.

To be spiritual as a parent, according to Levin, is to be constantly amazed. "To quote the words of Prof. Abraham Joshua Heschel, a great teacher of our age, our goal should be to live life in radical amazement. He would encourage his students to get up in the morning and look at the world in a way that takes nothing for granted. Everything is phenomenal; everything is incredible; never treat life casually. To be spiritual is to be amazed.

"I see this as part of my fatherhood, to transmit this to my kids, to live each day as if it's a whole lifetime."

One of the men in my living room, exploring the notion of radical amazement, said the only miracles he had ever experienced were the births of his children.

But it seems to me that childbirth is only the first of the miracles. Each growth spurt, each burst of consciousness in my sons, is another miracle. Even my eleven-year-old's preadolescence, his tentative pulling away, is a miracle of one more birth: Something more fully formed is emerging from the cocoon, all unfolding antennae and wet and crumpled wings, reaching back to me but emerging, emerging. . . . Is this any less a miracle than the one eleven years ago, when I first saw the slick crown of his head?

Spirituality is transmitted among generations, from parent to child, but also from child to parent. This interchange of spirit has received little attention from theologians or academics. With the exception of Harvard psychiatrist Robert Coles's book, *The Spiritual Life of Children,* this area remains ambiguous and unscrutinized. At least one study has shown that the degree of religious involvement of a young adult is related to how religious and how close the father is to the child, particularly the boy. (The same link is seen between mother and daughter.)[81]

In 1985 David Heller wrote of his study of the religious life of children. He found that, despite differences in age, sex, religion, and personality, all of the children he studied demonstrated "some similar processes in their expression of religious ideas."

Family imagery, Heller found, strongly influenced the deity imagery. "Family members interpret scripture and stricture for the children and act as the most influential socializers, so it is not surprising that God is closely asso-

ciated with fathers, mothers, and even grandparents."
One ten-year-old boy, for example, told Heller repeatedly
how God was "like Daddy" or "not like Daddy." An
eleven-year-old girl said, "God is like my grandfather.
He smiles a lot and fixes toys for you when you need
him to." Heller pointed out that the familial connection
to God "is not always an easy one for the children;
a parent's anger or depression has the potential to
blacken the image of God and trigger great religious
doubt."[82]

Some men with whom I spoke were uncomfortable with
the image of father as God; rather than the fundamental
religious paternalism they may have experienced at home
as children, they now seek a more transcendent spirituality
as fathers—let's call it *deep paternity*. Jesus says, "I and the
Father are one." In *Absent Fathers, Lost Sons*, Guy Corneau
writes:

> In addition to theological meanings we might take
> from Jesus's statement, another interpretation is that
> he had combined or reconciled the qualities of son and
> father within himself. He owned his authority and his
> competence and power . . . but he had also submitted
> himself and made himself vulnerable and open to dis-
> covering and being humiliated. He did not lose his
> sense of authority. He kept both authority and vulner-
> ability to the end. I think that is a paramount lesson
> of the crucifixion: I and the father are one—authority
> and discipleship are joined. . . .
>
> What we have to remember is that at any moment,
> whether we are seeing ourselves as the father or as
> the son, we are always both. So as an adult male we
> are fathers—whether we have sons or not.[83]

A man is born three times in his life, Corneau states:

> He is born of his mother, he is born of his father, and
> finally he is born of his own deep self. This last is the
> birth of his individuality. . . . Men's mourning for the
> unrealistic expectations they had of their fathers, and
> the solitude this mourning imposes upon them, are
> experiences that liberate them. Their suffering serves
> as an initiatory mutilation; it forces them to confront
> the reality of the objective world: the whole universe
> becomes their new home.[84]

The fifth dimension of fatherlove is by no means limited
or entirely attached to organized religion. Ultimately, fatherlove is a synthesis of spirit, village-making, and earthkeeping.

It offers us, as men, something larger than ourselves,
even if we do not have children of our own, even if our
children are gone from us. Despite loneliness and separation, we can offer fatherlove; that offering connects us with
the world and beyond.

On a plane a decade ago I met a Southern Pacific Railroad engineer who for many years had been a noncustodial
father and had been separated from his son. We were sitting beside each other on a jet somewhere over Texas,
heading for San Antonio in the night. We struck up a conversation, and he began to talk about freight trains and
fatherhood and running the rail route known as the
"Stormy."

"It's a scary run, goes from Tucson, Arizona, up to
Lordsburg, New Mexico, middle of nowhere, just some bar-
racks for railroad crews. Up there, the movie house burnt
down. There's just a bar and the railroad. This particular
run is one of the worst. You start in the desert, and then

suddenly you're up in the mountains and the trees. Sometimes it's snowing and lightning at the same time. The company says, 'If you can run a train in Stormy, you can run it anywhere.' We have runaways out there; so many derailments it's pathetic." He laughed. "One time the flagman threw red in my face. Had to stop a train eighty-five hundred tons and eighty-two hundred feet long. Like that."

The engineer was a big man with rough edges and gentle edges and scars that showed and scars that didn't. He pulled his knees up and scrunched around in a losing effort to fit himself to the jetliner's seat. He talked about "doin' the job."

He told me he ran two kinds of trains. "A dog, an all-night crawler, we're talking about eight or nine thousand feet of train slow and dangerous, and the other is a shooter, a hot dog—that's a fast one, an expedited train. Odds are, an engineer is going to hit somebody someday, and it won't be the engineer's fault. A housewife late to day care will try to run a crossing; a farmer half asleep will ram the side of the train; a clerk will lay his head on the track or stand between the rails, mesmerized by the headlight, and at the last minute just turn his back.

Part of the Stormy runs along Interstate 10, so he can look out the cab of his engine and see the twentieth century gaining on him, all those truckers leaning into the wind. "Sometimes they wave, and sometimes they flip me the bird," he said. "I'll tell you, the railroad employee is just a number, and that's the truth. There's still pride there, but self-pride. It's a private thing; you and the dispatcher know what you're doin', but the company doesn't. But that's the job. I'm an engineer, you know what I'm sayin'?"

He fell silent as the jet droned through the night.

"I get paid well, but I can tell you about heartbreak, brakemen going place to place because business is down. This brakeman, he's a good man, got a wife and three kids; he loves his job, and he goes where the money is. Goes three or four months without seeing her. They don't tell you about that stuff." Another long silence, but then his mood brightened. He sat up straight. "You know, when I'm goin' down those twin silver lines, when I see some kids in a housin' division wavin' and pullin' their arms down, 'Blow your horn, blow your horn,' I do it, cause they're dreamin'! I wish I had them up there in my arms.

"It's a dream they'll never do because society restricted them. Parents want them to be doctors or lawyers. I feel like I'm livin' a life for kids who don't know what adventure is because they're so restricted nowadays. They've got no place to play anymore, but a train goes by, and it's freedom going by, and I blow my horn for 'em and I laugh, I feel good inside. I've been in a place called Benson, Arizona; kids twelve, fourteen years old, and they come around the engine five or six times and I'll say, 'You want to come on here?' They say, 'Really?' And I feel damn good. Maybe I'm a crazy man, but give 'em some hope, give 'em something to dream about. There ain't much hope left."

Thinking of him now, I realize he was expressing fatherlove, albeit indirectly.

Years before, he had let his son ride on his lap and touch the controls that ran a ten-thousand-foot train, out to a coal plant near San Antonio, Texas.

"Last week, my boy told me that when he decided, at fourteen, to go with me for custody, that he remembered that. He said, 'My father considers me a human being.' You ask him that sometime, he'll tell you. I've told him about my life: You know how it feels to be on a train, in the engine, pulling eight thousand tons? You look back and say, 'Wow, I'm haulin' America's freight, I'm haulin' the economy. When you haul troops, armor, parts for jets, parts for the space shuttle, if we weren't there, guy, that stuff wouldn't be there. You look back, and you got Tristar wings that are going to go on some satellite somewhere, and you look back at that and you go, 'Wow, without me that wouldn't get where it's goin'.' You haul mail, and you look back and see the UPS trucks lined up, and all you see is somebody's paychecks, somebody's love letters, that wouldn't get there without you. It's got to be done. They've tried to kill my pride, but they haven't.''

And he talked about people who still jump freight trains. "The guys with the billy clubs aren't there anymore. I feel a man riding a freight is doing it for one of two reasons: He loves the railroad, or he's down and out. I've come across Mexicans, blacks, whites, college kids, I've smelled their stench in the middle of the summer, and in the middle of the winter I've found them under the floor in the engine, in the trapdoors under the valves, hidin' from the *migra*. *'¿Qué pasa?,* what's happenin'? They say, 'Ain't got no money.' I say, 'Fine. Don't touch nothin', you stay warm, just don't touch nothin'.' I find kids on there who are well-to-do; they just love the train; I say, 'Fine, just don't touch nothin'.' I let 'em ride.''

He stared out the window for a while. The lights of San Antonio were just below as the jet circled. The pilot turned the overhead lights off, and the jet approached the runway. The engineer was smiling in the dark.

"My boy is down there. He's comin' back home with me.''

If suffering is redemptive and if all things can be made new, as many believe, then a man can find his manhood, his fatherhood, and his spirituality at the same time. He can do this if he listens closely, as did Stan Hay.

In the beginning, Stan Hay was going to be somebody.

At forty-three, he is a relatively young man, but he hobbles a bit, lifting his knees with some effort, the result of gunshot wounds below the belt. Right now, he's sitting in the office of the community organizing group for which he works, down the street from the Backyard Barbecue, a hole-in-the-wall restaurant owned by his wife and sister-in-law. Hay washes dishes and cleans up.

When Hay was a boy growing up in Oakland, like many African-American men, he figured that sports was his ticket to . . . somewhere. He doesn't remember anyone telling him they admired him for who he was, only for who he would be.

One day, a scout for the Houston Colt 45s came to his door and told Stan's mother that he would be a famous baseball player someday. That's when the fear began. Maybe, he thought, he wouldn't make it; maybe he wouldn't be somebody, ever.

"During my first real fist fight, I learned that I was gifted at violence. When I went into a rage I didn't have to deal with being afraid, with not feeling like I could tell anybody about how frightened I was, didn't have to deal with anybody; they had to deal with me. I could just lose myself."

After a street brawl in 1965, he was sentenced at age seventeen to prison. He spent a year in Soledad. But his life was not without luck. A visiting coach from the University of Oregon saw him play football on the prison team. The coach worked for two years to obtain an early release for Hay and arranged a sports scholarship to the university.

Stan Hay was finally going to be somebody.

Then during a bar fight, a few weeks after he was re-

FatherLove

leased from prison, someone pointed a shotgun at him and shattered his ankle and his sports career.

Hay descended into ten years of hell. He sold and used hard drugs. Sometimes $50,000 a month would pass through his hands. He killed no one, but not, he says, from lack of trying. He was shot again, by police. He was severely burned when rival dope dealers blew up his house while he was alseep in bed. He was hospitalized for five months, then in 1975 returned to prison at San Quentin for three years. But some force beyond him, or within him, was already at work on Hay's spirit.

During this decade, the seventies, he kept a secret in the Oakland, California, hills. Every couple of weeks, during the periods he wasn't in prison or in the hospital, he would visit a woman named Nancy, a single mother with two kids. "None of my associates—I don't want to call them friends—knew about them." He kept his relationship with Nancy a secret to protect her and her children from his life, from the retribution of his enemies. He also did it to protect Nancy from her abusive ex-husband. And very slowly, he began to change.

At San Quentin, where Hay was feared, he found himself spending more and more time alone in his cell, avoiding the other men. "But one time we were having a tea talk in a cell, a bunch of us smoking pot and talking. This one guy was telling us how he had driven up into the Oakland hills with somebody he had known for fifteen years and stabbed him to death simply because he had the impression that the BGF (Black Guerrilla Family, a prison-based gang) wanted him dead.

"I wasn't really paying attention at first. And then I started to hear something in his voice, and I looked at this guy, he was maybe twenty-seven, and his face was glowing. He looked like he was about to have an orgasm, talk-

211

ing about how he was holding his friend, who was big and screaming, and how he stabbed him and how the blood got all over him.

"I'm thinking, this sucker is so sick that the only way he can validate himself is by snuffing somebody out, and that scared me."

What scared him most was the realization that there was a limit to his own violence. In prison, such a limitation could be lethal. That was when he began to avoid confrontation. Finally, completely, he was a nobody. And the fear in him began to turn like a shark; it came rushing up from beneath the bravado and the violence, and began to gain on him. In order to save himself, Stan Hay had to redefine manhood and find his fatherhood.

"One evening I was sitting in my cell alone," Hay remembers, "looking out through the bars and down a catwalk where the gun rail was and through a window. The sun was going down, and I could barely see a patch of water. There was still a little light on the water. And the stars looked like they were sitting right on top of the ocean. I was never into nature walks and that kind of stuff, but I was sitting there and— Do you ever want to do something, and you just get up and do it?

"I wanted to get up, go outside, and walk in what I was seeing. The more I thought about it, the more I wanted to do it and the more I realized I couldn't."

He vowed to get out and stay out. Released two years later, in 1980, he was caught up almost immediately in another misadventure. During a drug raid, he refused to keep his face to the wall, and as he tells it, police shot him in the legs and groin. "I almost lost my manhood. I remember the doctor telling me I better be glad it was a nine millimeter, because if it had been a thirty-eight, the bullet would have ripped it right off. I had four recontructive operations because my urethra was cut in half. There was a lot of muscle trauma, and every time they operated on me, it made more trauma. But I learned something. I learned at that point that I needed to leave Oakland."

Which he admits was something of an understatement.

No drugs had been found in the raid, so now, a free man, he married Nancy, the woman in the Oakland hills, and they moved to San Diego.

And he battled an old voice in his head. Whenever he got near alcohol or drugs, this voice would say, "Why not?" He attended Narcotics Anonymous meetings. The voice faded slightly. But Hay figures that his stepkids Kenya and John softened the voice more than NA.

As a boy and young man, Hay was admired for his potential to become a sports hero, though he never made it. As a drug dealer and prison inmate, he had been feared. Nancy loved the good man she believed he would one day become. But he says his stepkids were the first people to love him for who he was.

"I'd go out to the store, and John would say, 'Where are you going?' I'd say, 'Just to the store.' He'd say, 'I'm going with you.' This eight-year-old kid would grab my leg. He needed me. He needed a dad."

Yet the old voice continued to whisper. "I remember sitting in a park at four o'clock in the morning. Nobody in this park but me. I don't even think there was a bird in the park. I was crying. I had tried so hard, and here I was again, high on cocaine. I mean, I'd leave my house, not a problem in the world, to go to the store, and through a chain of events and a pattern of old habits, I'd find myself hours or days later, saying, 'What the hell happened?' I remember saying, 'Okay, God, here it is. If I have to be like this, I would rather not be here at all.' "

One day, he realized that his stepson had begun to mirror him. He saw this in the way the boy walked, with his hobbling gait. He saw it in the small patterns of conversation, and he saw it when, at age twelve, John began to be excessively aggressive.

"I realized that I still defined manhood as domination. I was subtly teaching my son that to be a man meant to be on top of something. With my wife, I would hear myself saying, 'Okay, that's it, we discussed it enough, you had your say, now here's my final answer.' With the kids, I'd hear myself saying, 'I don't need to explain this to you. You don't have a right to an explanation.' "

Stan can't pinpoint any particular time when this need to dominate began to fade, but over time he came to know that a man who dominates is usually dominated by his own fear, that a man who does not listen has nothing to say, that a man who has all the answers knows none of the questions.

And he began to hear a new voice. It would slip up the back of his neck and into his head. Instead of "Why not?" the new voice asked, " 'Why? Why do you need that stuff? What are you doing?' If I could have shut that sucker up or pushed it down, I probably would have. But see, I couldn't."

Today, Hay is a community organizer for the San Diego Organizing Project, which fights crime, and he has achieved a degree of heroism among his neighbors that had evaded him as an athlete and drug dealer.

His stepdaughter, Kenya, is twenty-one; John is twenty. They're doing fine. Hay understands that the mistakes he has made in his life have been imprinted on his wife and stepchildren. His new granddaughter, he says, is the first member of the family "not touched by the insanity of my past." At least not directly.

He pauses for a long time, rubs his fingers over his

scarred face. "I figure now that maybe a 'man' is just the end of 'human.' Or maybe that's too easy an answer."

Listening to Stan's story of suffering and redemption, I was struck by the ironies of his initiation and scarring.

Some men, involved in the men's movement, are increasingly interested in rediscovering or developing manhood initiation rites. Much of the talk, about male initiation, seems to me to be academic, intellectualized or romanticized, and yet there is some truth to the fact that our society, by ignoring the passage into manhood, does great damage to fatherhood and children. Stan had told a story of a different kind of initiation and almost ritualized scarring, an initiation going on right now, for many young men, in city after city.

Most of the reason for this negative initiation is that positive male role models are few and far between. Stan did have some adult males in his life, ones who attempted to offer him a way out. But as he learned, sports is a narrow ritual; village-building turned out to be far more fulfilling. But first, he submitted to something even greater than community.

"See, I believe that I started trying to change years and years ago and that I wasn't able to under my own power," he says. "I had to make a connection with something outside of myself. I call it God; you may call it what you want. But I must be able to talk to somebody. Believe me, there's things in my life that I've done that I'm not going to tell you, and I'm not going to tell my wife, or my mother, or nobody. Some things I just don't think that they're anybody's business or that there's a reason that anybody needs to know. But by the same token, I know I can't hold them all myself. I don't have the capacity, so I talk to God."

I had explained to him that I considered spirituality to be the fifth and final dimension of fatherhood.

He shook his head. "You say it's the fifth, but to me it's kind of the first because if I didn't have the spiritual contact or the spiritual involvement, I don't think that the other four would really matter," he said. "I wouldn't be able to do anything with my kids. I probably wouldn't be here. I know that because I tried so long to do it by myself. I don't know how right I am, but to me, a person who is nonspiritual tends to only see self, to operate from self."

Too many children are left to themselves and to the manipulations of media: Their initiation into adult society happens whether or not their fathers arrange it. They initiate themselves by imitating superstars. They are initiated through gangs or fraternities, where youths initiate youths into imitations of adult society. For decades, fraternity initiations have been something of a poor substitute for a father-son rite of passage. Some black fraternities have, for decades, ritualistically branded their initiates.

Journalist Sharon Griffin quotes one member of Omega Psi Phi describing how, two decades ago, his fraternity brothers branded the Greek letter Ω into his right arm, when he was a student at the University of New Mexico. He remembers the moment with absolute clarity. "It was like being baptized. Born again," he told Griffin. However bonded with their fellow members such men may continue to feel, fraternity initiations remain largely the initiation of youths by youths.

Guy Corneau describes how young people in our culture, like those in tribal cultures, "must go through a transition, an initiatory stage; they must explore the limit of their future identities." But our "ancestral initiation has been emptied of its content and of its participation in the sacred meaning of the universe."[85] He describes one people's ritual:

> The Australian aborigines . . . re-enact the initiate's original birth. They build a tunnel of branches and bushes, twenty or thirty feet in length, and require the boy to go into it. After a great deal of shouting and commotion, the initiate emerges from the other end of the tunnel, where he is welcomed with open arms and solemnly declared to be a man. He has been reborn through the body of man; he now possesses a new mind and a new body.[86]

Male intuition rituals in such cultures do not focus only on initiating boys into the world of men, but also into the world of parenthood. Kyle Pruett, author of *The Nurturing Father*, describes *couvade*, a ritualized custom observed in some South Pacific cultures:

> The expectant father undergoes a simulated pregnancy and delivery. He enters the men's hut late in his mate's pregnancy, takes to bed when she begins pre-labor, and stays there throughout her labor and delivery. With intense, hysterical writhing and moaning, twisting and turning, he simulates female labor in graphic detail. . . . the man is easing his spouse's pain, not vicariously but actually, and by so doing he is protecting his wife and his offspring from harm.[87]

This doesn't sound all that different from the rhythmic Lamaze breathing that I shared with my wife. This may be the modern initiation ritual that will connect many men of my generation to their children in ways that enter the spiritual realm. The transport that my wife and I felt during these hours and moments was a ritualistic, and to us a spiritual, event—a tunneling transport, heart to heart—a blanking out of everything except the connection of two souls on behalf of a third.

Why don't we teach young boys that fatherhood makes you high? Why do we transmit to them news mainly of breadwinning and the chores, and ignore the spiritual transport, the blisteringly beautiful moments of fatherhood?

Are we embarrassed to talk about this?

Fathers, when invited to talk about these things, often described blinding moments of realization: sitting with their sons or daughters in their arms and suddenly realizing that they would do *anything*, lay down their lives, jump in front of a car, anything to protect their children. Or they described walking with their child or looking at him or her in the rear-view mirror, and suddenly realizing *this is my child* and feeling an overwhelming sense of awe, and at these instants of the spirit, tears came to their eyes.

As a ritual initiation of young men in our culture, the bar mitzvah remains. By Jewish tradition, a boy on his thirteenth birthday becomes personally responsible for his actions and accepts the laws of his religion. This ceremony introduces him, lifts him, into the world of adults. But Christianity, traditionally father-oriented (the Father, the Son, and the Holy Spirit), is curiously reluctant to address the transcendent spirituality of fatherhood.

Many churches describe the ideal father as the spiritual leader of the family (a limiting, if not enslaving, prescription for both the father and mother), but seldom address the pain and pleasure of the transcendent spiritual moments of fatherhood. Even the religious leaders assembled in my living room, most of them, had difficulty rising above a discussion of the daily administrations of fatherhood. It seems to me that the fading of fatherhood in our culture has less to do with the lost powers of paternalism than with the great silence about the spiritual payoff of fatherhood.

Our churches, in their efforts to address the problems of children, offer parenting classes. But these courses are often gender-free, child-specific, and oddly clinical. Where is the discussion of the transcendent? Unless this aspect of fatherhood—deep paternity—is shared among fathers, and mothers, and passed on to sons, there is little likelihood that fatherhood itself will be treated with any reverence, let alone aspired to as a state of consciousness by young men with other options for intoxication.

Perhaps churches could develop new traditions, or rediscover old ones; they could offer parenting classes not only to parents, but to future parents. Whether these courses are taught in a coeducational style or are focused on fathering or mothering, there would be value in providing some kind of graduation ritual. Perhaps these courses should begin before puberty.

One rite-of-manhood model is Avance (meaning "get ahead"), a church-based, government- and corporate-funded retreat in San Antonio, where young Latino men participate in traditional American Indian ceremonies and take vows of nonviolence and responsible fatherhood. As Nina Easton reports in the *Los Angeles Times Magazine*, Avance founder Gloria Rodriquez originally taught only women. "But she quickly sensed that their newfound skills and confidence threatened their husbands and boyfriends. Rather than risk breaking up families, Avance opened its doors to men, who attend regular classes on child development and parenting techniques."[88]

Big Brothers, the Boy Scouts, Indian Guides, and other similar organizations could offer their own rites of passage. Sports can also offer a collective initiation. Participating fathers could, in fact, be initiated themselves, through education about child development and about the spiritual fragility of the young members of their teams, and, as well, about their role on the field as spiritual guides—often to fatherless boys.

Gregory Vogt and Stephen Sirridge suggest that this initiation can be accomplished by a father or male mentor arranging a gathering of several generations of men, at key points in the boy's life, particularly in early and late adolescence. He suggests that, for a son, a father can gather his own father, his uncles, and his brothers. These gatherings would honor the boy in some way and recognize his growth and his potential. "This could serve as an exciting and healing revelation for all of the men involved," write Vogt and Sirridge. "It would offer a sense of continuity, family, and regeneration of manhood and maleness."[89]

Other meaningful rituals can emerge naturally, allowing a certain magic to come forth. For example, a father and son or a male mentor might return regularly to a favorite fishing or hiking spot, or a coffee house—where they talk. The setting might represent some area of special interest of the father (in my case, fishing) or the son (in my older son's case, comic conventions). Regularly repeating these experiences offers the father and the son a doorway into each other's world, a two-way initiation.

Men can also initiate their sons and other young men into the world of work—not only the methods of work, but the reasons for work—by being together side-by-side in the yard or the home office or by going into the workplace and talking about the passionate or spiritual reasons for working. Men at home or in the workplace can also create an environment of apprenticeship for boys and young men. Although most corporations do not recognize the value of mentoring, older employees can guide young people into the adult world, especially if they communicate that work can be connected to something larger than ego or salary. None of these rituals need be overbearing; sometimes all a child needs is to be left alone, but nearby.

Adult rituals and ceremonies for boys and young men can become a kind of male womb in which the boy's own deep paternity has a chance to grow. Education is the one initiation rite that our society does, generally, accept; yet, public education neglects or avoids the discussion of parenting, particularly fatherhood. We need a community curriculum to link schools to churches, synagogues, and other places of worship, as well as secular organizations concerned with child development and parenting skills. We need a new emphasis on mentoring in elementary and secondary education; in some school systems, that is already occurring, with male teachers offering support over a number of years. Such attention to young men could not only help them become good fathers in the future, but also help now to fill the male void in families headed by single mothers. At its best, such mentoring can be, indirectly, spiritual.

In addition to helping young men learn more about the spiritual aspects of fathering, places of worship must do more to build a community of support for fathers and their families, within the church and beyond. They might begin by examining their own family policies.

"A church I served at in Texas objected to fathers on the church staff who came in late. They were dropping their kids off at day care," one church worker told me. "The administration said being flexible isn't the way the working world works and that we've got to be more businesslike, whatever that means."

Think what could be accomplished if tens of thousands of churches became role models by treating their own parent-employees better. And what if, from the pulpits, ministers (usually men) expressed fatherlove by recognizing and honoring the businesses that help families with their company policies?

Churches can also do more to help intact marriages stay that way. As David Blankenhorn points out, the Catholic Church already offers impressive marriage programs. Until quite recently, however, many other Christian churches had drifted away from an emphasis on marriage and family. A further reemphasis, he suggests, could be drawn from a very old tradition. During the Baptism ceremony in many churches, parents traditionally stand with the baby; members of the congregation pledge before one another and before God to act as an extended family for that child. They might also pledge to support the mother and the father.

"When I was a child, the people in my church remembered me: sent me cards on my birthday, watched out after me in often small but significant ways," says Blankenhorn. "Yet so much of that has been forgotten. Here we have the potential for a strong supportive community for the parents and child, a potential to relearn and build upon this old tradition." One of the recruiting secrets of the growing "megachurches" is that they have recognized that young parents need help and support to navigate the larger environment, unfriendly and hostile to children and families. "The return to an emphasis on helping families doesn't have to start with the minister or the rabbi but with the people in the pew," says Blankenhorn.

Traditionally, the focus of parental support has been on

the mother. The men's movement has stimulated some churches to focus more on men's support groups. Rev. Dick Thompson's church, for example, now offers a men's group, fathering seminars, and a fathering retreat.

It is an important spiritual enterprise for us to think back on our family journeys, to tell our fathers' stories and our stories and our children's stories. This is one way to discover the hand of God in our lives.

One guy came up to me, after a session, and told me about the suicide of one of his children, how that had completely changed his life. How some things didn't matter to him any more and others had become vital. Men in these groups who have been laid off from work, who have lost so much of what they had counted on, who were utterly shaken—these men often express a new openness to talk and share what really matters. These men tend to be neither young nor old. What I am about to say is too simplistic, but there are two kinds of men, men who are aware of the *wall* and men who aren't. There is the man who shows no emotion and will not weep, the man with no sense of history, who does not even see the wall. This man tends to be younger or older. And there is the man, who tends to be nearing or at middle age, who is conscious that he is approaching the wall; he's smashing his face into this wall of increasingly inappropriate expectations, rules, and roles for men.

These men are ready to reconceive their fatherhood and manhood. They're ready to go through the wall.

Rituals in the home can also help a father experience his spirituality, as well as nurture his children's. Steven Bayme believes that religious Jews and Christians should bring back the Sabbath and that all people, religious or not, can create a kind of personal Sabbath—a family Sabbath. By that, he means a day focused entirely on the family and the spirit, when work is stopped, the TV turned off, and the heart turned inward.

Bayme is director of the Jewish Communal Affairs Department of the American-Jewish Committee in New York, and director of the Institute on the Jewish Family. He describes himself as a person "who strongly believes in the power of tradition." He is critical of an older attitude toward children in the synagogue, "that they should be seen and not heard," and praises the efforts of many synagogues to incorporate children more into services. He also points to the growing number of Jewish parents who are rediscovering the rituals of the Sabbath as a way, in an increasingly hectic world, to spend concentrated time with their children.

"I am a father," says Bayme, "with three traditional obligations: to teach my child a living; to teach him survival skills; and to transmit Jewish tradition."

Regarding the latter, he says, "The act of studying Jewish text together, which is part of the Sabbath ritual, accomplishes several objectives. First, it is a statement to children that the Jewish tradition is still relevant; second, it sends out the message that the family is the setting where spiritual values are passed on from one generation to the next; third, it's a bonding experience." Bayme quotes Abraham Joshua Heschel, who called the Sabbath "sacred time," a one-day retreat from worldly pressures and influences.

"In my work I keep very late hours and travel frequently," says Bayme. "My kids will often be in bed when I get home. The amount of time we spend during the week is unfortunately quite minimal. . . . But the Sabbath is a time to recharge our batteries.

"My children look forward to the Sabbath as a time of joy. On Friday night we have a dinner surrounded by Jewish rituals; this is an opportunity for extended conversation, with no pressure to meet any deadlines, a time when we have friends over. We ban television on the Sabbath. We allow no external intrusions. All entertainment must be self-generated. If the weather is nice, we go out for a walk. I really look forward to this time.

"On Saturday we go to the synagogue. There, children are treated differently than in the past; now the synagogue is a place of celebration for families." For Bayme the Sabbath (or any ritualized, regular day of rest) must have a dramatically different texture than the rest of the week. "This is a time to focus on the internal quality of our lives. This is what Heschel meant by sacred time."

For Jews the Sabbath begins at sundown on Friday and ends at sundown on Saturday. For most Christians the Sabbath is Sunday. Until the late 1950s, so-called blue laws required stores to be closed on Sunday in many states. While no lobby is rushing to bring back those laws, some mainstream Christian leaders are discussing how to revive the idea of a day of rest.

One friend, a Methodist, says, "It's so easy to get caught up in the rush, even on Sunday, when I'm so busy teaching Sunday school, volunteering with a literacy program, going to district and regional church meetings, and coming into the office to put in a few hours of work. You almost need a formal ritual to break that pattern." This woman has decided that Saturday is her personal Sabbath.

Such time doesn't need to be specifically religious but does need to be sacred. During the summer, my wife and

I decided that we would take our kids to the beach one morning a week. We left the blankets and chairs in the car trunk. Every week we jumped in the car and headed for the surf, leaving deadlines, homework, and TV behind. Going to the beach may not be your idea of a Sabbath, but for a while it was ours. The key was the ritual. Without that, the summer would have disappeared while we waited for a convenient time to go to the beach.

Another wall that places of worship must face is that which exists between their institutions and the world of family policy: the building of the village.

Churches must reach beyond their own walls to weave a support system for all families and all fathers, whether or not they're considered religiously correct. Many churches and other places of worship are beginning to do just that, and in the process they are challenging their own institutional isolation within the larger society.

"The church can't wait for the community to come and say 'We need your help,' " says Rev. Dan Meyer-Abbott, a Methodist minister in San Diego. "We need to go out and ask how we can help families in stress. As Martin Luther King said, 'We can't be the taillights of society; we've got to be the headlights.' "

Beyond church and home and the village, nature offers a spiritual community for fathers. But the male mystique—the ethic of dominance—destroys men's ties to the earth, says men's movement activist Andrew Kimbrall. The male mystique, he says, embodies the view of seventeenth century British philosopher John Locke that that which is "left wholly to nature is called, as indeed it is, waste." But true fatherkeeping is akin to earthkeeping. If men are to recapture a true sense of stewardship and husbandry "and affirm the seedbearing, creative capacity of the male," as Kimbrall puts it, they must become earthfathers and earthkeepers.[90]

This was the meaning of Steve Darden's ritual on the mountain.

I remember my father's connection to land and water. In the spring in the Midwest, box turtles would crowd the country roads in some kind of sexually stimulated migration, and puritanical cars would flatten them. Now and then on the road you'd see a spinner, a box turtle on its back, clipped by a car ahead, spinning so fast that it was a blur. My father would slam on the brakes, and my mother would jump out and save the spinner. The car floor beneath my feet would fill up with box turtles. We would take them home and keep them for the summer in a chicken-wired hole in the backyard, a turtle pit my father had dug for me, and now, I understand, for him.

And I remember, earlier, spending hours at my father's feet, seeing his shoes sink into the dirt of the garden; I can still see the dirt dried on his shoes. I remember now, my eyes riveted to my father's feet as he crushed the flames of a small grass fire. And looking up, I see him wearing an army coat, a baseball cap; he is in his early twenties, but he seems to me at this moment to be the oldest man on earth. The only man on earth. I remember, too, laying down sod with him, in a rush, as a thunderstorm approached; and hiking in the woods with him; and, of course, fishing with him, gliding silently among a stand of dead trees left there after the lake's water had been raised and then dropped, watching him cast delicately between the trees.

These memories were formed long before my father's life turned, but they create a kind of spiritual window for me, to nature, to another world beyond nature, and I hope to pass this sense of wonder on to my own sons.

Part Three

Conclusion

VIII

Fatherkeeping

WE CAN CONVERSE ALL WE WANT ABOUT THE MOST RE-
warding dimensions of fatherhood, of spirit and time and
community and work and nurturing, but without a new
national commitment to fatherhood, this talk will amount
to so much middle-class, middle-age chest-beating. Too
many young Americans begin and end their experience of
fatherhood at its most rudimentary dimension.

In Baltimore I visited a group of young men, ages sixteen
to twenty-three, the participants in the nonprofit Young
Fathers Program. If there is hope for the young fathers in
this program, there is hope for middle- and upper-class
fathers to overcome the pain and lack of fathering that they
may have experienced, and to learn to be better fathers to
their children.

The young men in this program described the revolving
door of sex, drugs, and child support, and how this program was trying to help them find a way out.

Listen to Charles (I have changed their names), twenty-three, an unwed father supporting his child alone. His son's mother was killed a couple of years ago. "By gunshot," he says. He won't go into the details. Listen to high school dropout Randall, nineteen, who has "four kids or maybe five." And Hawk, who has sown the seed for seven offspring. He counts to himself. "Four moms."

Are you proud of being dads? I asked.

"It's something that happens," said Randall.

"I'm back like twenty-five hundred dollars in child support, back three months from when I lost my job," said Hawk. "Sometimes you can sweet-talk your way around the system. I see a white guy who owed more money get off easy. The black judge is harder on blacks. Black judge says, 'It's a damn shame,' because you're black."

Hawk is smart, quick. Later, he talked movingly of wanting to be a good father, though he's not sure what that means beyond bringing in money. During his peak six months, Hawk made $20,000 selling drugs. He insists that one of his motivations for dealing was "to pay child support and stay out of jail. Couldn't find a job." In fact, all of the young men said they've dealt drugs, and all of them said that child support was one of the motivators.

By this lame logic, I said, toughening child-support laws will create more drug dealers, right?

They nodded.

Tyrone Furman leaned forward and said, "You've got to understand the revolving door." Furman is the program coordinator for the Young Fathers Program. He is married and a college graduate. At thirty-one he has become a kind of father to these younger men.

In Maryland, he explained, welfare mothers receive Aid to Families with Dependent Children grants through the state. One of the stipulations of receiving the grant is that if the mother is unmarried, divorced, or separated, she agrees to turn over any money she receives from the father to the state. Young men are required to pay their bill to the state when, as state legalese phrases it, they are "emancipated," which means turning eighteen or maintaining themselves outside the homes of their parents or guardians. Consequently, a sixteen-year-old could be required to pay child support to the state. After the initial court order, the bill can mount up quickly. While Furman believes that the state should be aggressive in pursuing child support, he points to the bind in which fathers with little prospect for employment find themselves.

Charles joined in, speaking slowly, as if teaching economics to a particularly dim student. "If you sell drugs for like a week, make a good four thousand, give two thousand for child support, that keeps you up for at least eight months, if you don't get caught dealing."

"It's easy money, they can keep the court off their backs," said Furman. "One twenty-three-year-old in my program owes nine thousand dollars in child support. Most of them say, 'I want to find a way to get out of this, get a job.' They get a bill from the state for one thousand to two thousand dollars, and if they don't pay, they're going to jail. The father sits in there for three to six months. When he gets out, the weeks he's been in jail are added to his bill. He's got another court date coming up in another four or five months, and he'll probably be back to jail." Even if these young men can find jobs, most will be low-skilled, part-time positions, and they won't be able to keep up with their child-support payments anyway.

Furman wants the government to offer men real jobs instead of jail, and apprenticeship programs to link them with positive male role models. He points out that it costs about $1,500 a month to imprison a man who hasn't been paying, say, $160 a month in child support.

Surely, I suggested, such a punitive system must deter teenagers from procreating. Hawk shrugged. Charles rolled his eyes.

"Kids here start having real sex at eleven or twelve," said Randall. "No jobs, nothin' to do, we got a lot of time on our hands."

"Kids don't see the problem," added Hawk. "They see the dealers in cars and gold. Really, dealers are the smartest persons in the neighborhood. But they're killing their own people. It's one thing when a white man don't care about you, but when a black person don't care about you, who's going to care about you? Anyhow, I see myself in jail sometime soon for child support. Hell, yeah. I got a little cell waiting for me."

Hawk's eyes flickered, the light in them went dark. Then he smiled. He was carefully dressed, articulate, with an edge. Like the other young men, he has dealt drugs in the past to pay his child-support payments, to avoid jail. He knows that selling drugs hurt people. "I changed. I changed a hundred percent."

Why?

"I don't know. Because of Tyrone. He slowed me down."

Tyrone Furman's program, sponsored in part by a non-profit organization, Friends of the Family in Annapolis, offers young fathers counseling and education in parenthood, employment, and child support. The fathers are referred to the program by government offices, courts, prisons, and word of mouth on the streets. The program offers these young men positive male role models: the program's staff, volunteers, and visiting community leaders.

"I don't listen to Tyrone," huffed Randall, turning his

cap around backward. "I listen to nobody since I was on the road when I was fourteen. Somebody tells me I'm going to get hit by a car, I'm still going to walk in the street to see if that car's going to hit me."

Then why is he participating in Tyrone's fathering program?

He shrugged. "Can't stay away, for some reason. But I'm listening to my conscience. I ain't listening to Tyrone. Trust me."

What was it about Tyrone that reached Hawk?

"He's big and nice," said Hawk. "He isn't big and evil. We met when we was working at the same furniture outlet. He was my friend. I went off and was dealing, but later he comes creepin' around my sister-in-law, before he got married, and he starts telling me, 'Come help me, do whatever.' He's the type of person that can get under your skin, make you think about things."

"I knew there were some good bones in Hawk," said Tyrone.

Hawk figures that of the seven kids he has sired, three will survive through their twenties. Based on the known mortality rate of young inner city black males, he's about right. He doesn't want to leave his neighborhood. He wants to be a community worker, like Tyrone.

And they all want to be good fathers.

"Sitting home, just sitting back thinking, thoughts come to your mind," said Randall, turning his hat back around. "It's gotta be God talking to you. It's gotta be God."

What kind of thoughts?

"Thoughts. . . . I'd just be sitting down thinking, and it just popped into my head, 'You got to get out and do something with your life. You can't just sit around here and do nothing.' "

Then Randall leaned over the tape recorder and said,

"Here's what I say. All fathers should look forward with confidence and no regrets. Concentrate on what they owe the world, not what the world owes them, and help those that help themselves. Act as if everything's dependent on you, and pray as if everything's dependent on God."

Do programs like this work? We don't know the answer yet, primarily because the approach is so new. Until quite recently, teenage fathers were almost completely overlooked, treated as outsiders, receiving none of the attention that sometimes is shown, by schools, community organizations, and government toward the teenage mother and child.

"At least the court now has a program it can refer young dads to instead of slapping them in jail," says Tamela Brumwella, a Maryland child support enforcement officer and a circuit court liaison with Furman's program. "All these years we've had services for the mom: social service stipends, state-sponsored classes in parenting skills, programs to make sure the mom gets to the doctor. We need all of those services and more for moms, but dads have been ignored." Brumwella, who worked previously with a rural program helping mothers, adds, "I've seen all these dads going from job to job, with no education or skills. Finally Tyrone's program came along. We've got to make more efforts like this. We can't keep neglecting fatherhood and expect improvement in the lives of children."

The privately funded Responsive Fathers Program at the Philadelphia Children's Network takes a similar approach. Young unmarried dads become better fathers and mates by receiving counseling services and job search assistance.

Participants, who range in age from sixteen to twenty-six, meet in group sessions once a week and discuss child rearing, male-female relationships, the job market, and self-esteem. Young fathers are referred to the program from hospitals, community centers, probation offices, or by word of mouth. The bureaucratic public assistance system discourages fathers from family involvement, but this can be reversed. "You have many fathers declared absent when they are actually present. People think they're just making babies and don't have any feelings attached to that act. Everyone says, 'We want you to be a responsible father,' but we give them nothing to be responsible with," according to director Thomas J. Henry.[91]

Charles Ballard, who runs the Teen Fathers Program in Cleveland, says he asked a group of fifteen boys how many were fathers. Only two raised their hands. When he asked how many had babies, fourteen hands went up. "They just don't think like fathers," Ballard says. "They don't connect pregnancy with marriage or husbanding or fatherhood." At least 65 percent of his clients never really knew their own fathers. "No man has ever touched their lives except a policeman," he says, "and he was approaching them with a gun or a billy club in his hand."[92]

The Cleveland program offered vocational services, counseling, and prenatal and parenting classes to nearly four hundred teenage fathers and prospective fathers in eight U.S. cities. After two years, more than eight in ten young fathers reported having daily contact with their children; seventy-four percent said they contributed to the child's financial support. And nearly ninety percent maintained a relationship with the mother, whom they had typically not seen for two years. At the end of the program, sixty-one of the young men had found jobs; forty-six of those who had dropped out of school had resumed their education. Progress is possible.[93]

Just as in recent years the emphasis of social service programs has shifted from the automatic removal of children from abusive homes to the more preventive approach of family preservation, we must develop a father preservation campaign. Rather than shaping future public and private policy primarily on the assumption that a fatherless society is inevitable, we must make a national and cultural commitment to fatherkeeping.

We need an ongoing effort to support and nurture good fatherhood, not only for low-income parents but also for fathers at all economic levels. More fathering courses should be offered by schools, churches, YMCAs, corporate personnel departments, and private programs. Some hospitals, for example, now offer classes designed to promote the bond between father and infant, and to teach parenting skills to fathers. Another example, as mentioned earlier, is a program based in San Diego called Dads U, which creates a forum for fathers to exchange experiences and gather information about parenting. Paul Lewis, president of Family University and founder of Dads U, says, "I tell men, if you don't want to do it for yourselves, do it for your kids. I find that most dads, including noncustodial fathers, want to do what is right for their kids, but they need help knowing what the right thing is." Lewis's goal is to train and field a hundred dads who would teach fathering courses across America.

But the existence of a few scattered father-teaching programs is not enough. The very nature of our institutions must be transformed.

FatherLove

Society tends to view change as something that happens at a personal level or through national legislation. But a vast region exists between those two extremes: the institutions in which we all live and work—the hospitals where our children are born and are cared for when they're ill, churches, synagogues, social service agencies, schools. Unless these institutions become family-friendly and father-friendly, no amount of reactive programs will do the job that must be done.

The most important institution that must change is the workplace. In partnership, men and women must work for equal pay for equal work; job sharing; flexible working hours; a provision for employees to work at home; family ties time—a few hours available each month, preferably paid, to volunteer or visit schools, day care, or elder care facilities; time off for family emergencies; temporary emergency care for those days when an employee's regular arrangements fail; company assistance with child care; family leave and other family-friendly policies.

Among the most effective pioneers in this area is James Levine, the father of two children and director of the Fatherhood Project, headquartered in New York, a national clearinghouse of information about fatherhood and a long-term research project. The program helps some of the nation's largest and most influential companies become more family-friendly and father-friendly. Participating companies include Apple Computer, Merrill Lynch, American Express, Time-Warner, Ortho Pharmaceutical, and Bausch & Lomb. "We've found little differences in fathers due to class or ethnicity," he said. "In inner-city Baltimore or on the thirty-seventh floor of a Fortune 500 company, the diction may be different, but the emotions and the needs are pretty much the same."

The inspiration for the project came during the late sixties when, as a young Amherst graduate, Levine taught preschool in Oakland, California. There, he was surprised to encounter subtle but daunting cultural and institutional resistance to fatherhood.

"I kept getting asked a question that none of the women at the school were ever asked: What do you really do? I had been sympathetic to the women's movement, but this was an epiphany," he recalls. "A light bulb went off. Growing up, I had always cared for kids. I was just one of those guys who helped out children in the lower grades. So why didn't people consider caring for children to be man's work?" Levine was subsequently hired by the Ford Foundation to help them determine how to spend their money on child care. "I was struck during all our discussions that child care was continually defined as a woman's issue. Of course, I was not naive enough to think that there were loads of men out there taking care of kids, but the foundation people and child-care advocates were acting as if men were an invisible species. Our culture will never solve this problem if it keeps asking the wrong question. We need to ask: How do we address family needs, not only a mother's needs?"

He first proposed creating the Fatherhood Project in 1978. Foundations were less than enthusiastic, but in 1980 the movie *Kramer vs. Kramer* was released. In the film, Dustin Hoffman portrayed a father facing the challenges of parenting alone. Suddenly foundations were eager to finance Levine's efforts to change company cultures. He began conducting seminars and focus groups at workplaces; he found that some institutions are ripe for change and may not even know it.

• We must identify and tell stories about father-friendly companies and programs. An accelerated effort should be made to measure the success rate of programs that teach or support fatherhood, or involve fathers in the education of children. And we need to widely publicize those companies that are father-friendly and show how individual men can make a difference. Levine believes that media should pay more attention to these companies. For example, many magazines have published articles describing great companies for working mothers; few have focused on good companies for working fathers.

• The workplace must create ways for fathers to mentor fathers and young men. Levine prefers to use the word "coach" rather than mentor. "The word *mentor* makes it sound like you're up on a pedestal," he says. "A coach is simply someone who brings out the talent in someone else. The first step to coaching is acknowledgment, to pay attention. There are so many kids who get no attention from anyone, and there is so much father hunger out there. I have a guy who works in my program, a former drug addict who has some talent; but he also suffers a terrible lack of social skills, particularly around women. One day I sat him down alone, and later, I asked several women from my staff to join us. We had a tough conversation with this guy about his unacceptable behavior and how he could improve it." One woman said later that if anyone had talked to her like that she would have never returned. "But he came back to the office on the following Monday and thanked me," says Levine. "This boy had lost his father at an early age. He said nobody had ever cared enough to talk to him like that; they had just assumed he was an unsalvageable jerk."

Such confrontations with future or current fathers may not be appropriate in every setting, but male mentoring programs could make a real difference.

New York City offers the City-as-School program for youngsters who are not succeeding in the traditional school system. As part of the program, young men and women are placed in jobs as interns and apprentices. "Some of these teenagers work in our office," says Levine. "This is one way, an important way, for me as a father, as a man, and as a professional to care for the next generation. I'm convinced that such coaching has powerful results. One boy was being pressured by his family to get married at a young age and start having babies. The Responsive Fathers Program in Philadelphia invited me to a meeting and asked if I had any associates who I would like to bring with me. I said, yes, I had one. "I took this young guy with me. We stayed in a fancy hotel. He got to hear other professionals speak, and we got to hear other young men tell their stories. This had a tremendous impact on him. Suddenly he realized: 'I'm not alone. It's not just Jim telling me this stuff about fatherhood; there's a whole world out there.' "

• We must identify and challenge cultural resistance to fatherhood within institutions. One barrier to more flexibility for parents and children is the importance placed by companies on "face time," the assumption that the more hours a worker is visibly present on the job, the more successful the worker is. "No matter how many hours of face time he puts in at work, a father who is worried about his children at home is unlikely to be fully productive," says Levine. This is also true of women, but we do not tend to think of fathers as worried working parents.

In order for such assumptions to be challenged, they must first be the topic of open, and probably organized, conversation within the institution.

"A decade ago, we were lucky if two or three men showed up at one of our company seminars and group discussions," says Levine. But during the past decade, especially since 1990, he has detected increasing acceptance of fatherhood within corporations and other institutions. "So many men showed up for our focus groups at Apple in 1990, that we had to add groups. If we had gone to Apple ten years earlier, we wouldn't have gotten the time of day," he says. When Apple announced its own family care initiative in 1991, the company devoted an entire page of its in-house newsletter to fathers, sending the message that the company's family policies applied to men, not only to women. The Apple newsletter described how the typical corporate culture assumes that women, but not men, should balance work and family. Apple announced that it would now encourage fathers and mothers to share responsibility for rearing children; the company would offer flexibility to both parents. That year, 1991, the first man asked for and took family leave; within three months, two other men in the division had also requested paternity leave.

• Even those institutions whose mission it is to care for and help children—churches, hospitals, schools—must examine their own policies and attitudes toward parenting and fatherhood. In the area of early childhood education, for example, the Fatherhood Project's research has found that some of the strongest resistance to father involvement is from women who work in the field. "When we discussed their resistance to fathers, they would say, 'Yes, we know we should get fathers more involved,' but they were making little effort to do that," he says. This resistance is understandable: Many of the women who work in early childhood education have been abandoned or abused by men, and they have seen their children disappointed by men. Nonetheless, the subtle resistance to men working with children "is emblematic of the attitude among many helping institutions: hospitals, mental health settings, schools. My point is not to blame women. We must surface the feelings of women and men and give voice to their ambivalence, as a first step to becoming partners." Levine believes that men must become more involved in early childhood education, at home as well as in preschool programs. He is currently creating a national training and technical assistance program for father involvement, targeting Head Start and other early childhood education programs. As he says, "We must begin everywhere at once. There isn't one entry point for change but many."

The role of primary and secondary education is crucial, but schools should be challenged to place much more emphasis on the dimensions and importance of fatherhood. Schools that offer family-life courses must place an equal emphasis on boys and girls, and a new approach is needed in many pregnancy prevention and sex-education courses.

"A major reason teenage pregnancy prevention programs are not more effective is because instructors, counselors, and other service providers often seem not to understand that when it comes to sex, boys and girls are different," says Karen J. Pittman of the Children's Defense Fund. "Even coeducational sexuality programs typically are packaged for adolescent females rather than males, despite research suggesting girls already know more about sex than boys do." Sex education may, therefore, unconsciously reinforce society's double standard of sexual behavior.

"Rather than assume that, since boys can't get pregnant, they don't care," writes Pittman, more attention should be paid to adolescent male attitudes toward employment "and other 'manhood' perceptions" that affect male sexuality. "While this 'whole adolescent' approach may be more important for boys than girls, current services tend to interpret 'whole adolescent' as 'whole girl.' These programs should be packaged differently to reach young men. . . . Given the societal emphasis on the father as provider, it is not surprising to hear some experts argue that, in many ways, improving young males' life options should be the first line of defense against teenage pregnancy."

What should be done to help boys and young males delay sexual activity and pregnancy? The Children's Defense Fund suggests the following key points:

• Increase their knowledge about sexual activity and its possible consequences, as well as their knowledge about how to avoid these consequences.

• Increase their ability to make mature decisions about sexual behavior by providing general counseling services, including forums for male-only, coed, and parent/child discussions.

• Foster the use of male contraceptive methods.

• Change the link between sex and manhood by showing positive alternative images of what it means to be a man. This can be done by providing positive role models, starting public education campaigns, changing current images in the media, and fostering concerted discussions and group counseling about alternative views of manhood.

• Strengthen the link between pregnancy and the responsibilities of parenthood, specifically by improving the current legal systems for paternity establishment and child support enforcement. In addition, according to the Children's Defense Fund, "there is a need to help all young men, but particularly disadvantaged young men, have positive life options and a real sense of a future. This is important because it gives them clear and compelling reasons to delay parenthood. It also allows them to believe that if they delay parenthood now, they will be able to better parent in the future."

One successful program is the "No Deposit, No Return" project, in Evanston, Illinois, operated by one of the non-profit Family Focus programs in the Chicago metropolitan area. The project helps young men understand what it means to be a father too soon, according to Delores Holmes, director of Family Focus Evanston. Between 1985 and 1989, Family Focus tracked twenty-five high school athletes at Evanston Township High School, a school with a high teen pregnancy rate. Over the four years, these young men attended parenting responsibility and sex education sessions at the Family Focus center. To remain on athletic teams, the young men were required to maintain adequate grades—and the requirement was enforced.

"We emphasized two themes: One was that they aren't all going to become professional athletes; if they do not deposit something in their heads now, they'll have nothing in their hands later. The second theme was sexual responsibility, the rights and responsibilities of fathering a child," says Holmes. Two male coordinators, one a new father himself, held sessions on parenting. "One of the realizations we had was that the boys need a more spiritual approach to this subject," says Holmes. "More than reading a book, they need to listen to men to talk about the importance of their seed, the realities of fathering, and what it means to be a teen parent. We also found that boys, when they're approached in this way, are just as eager to learn about parenting responsibilities as girls. Sometimes more eager." After four years, eighteen of the young men remained in the program; all eighteen graduated from high school, seventeen went on to college and none, while in high school, became fathers of children.

School-based clinics will also be an important part of any approach designed to reinvolve males in family responsibility. These clinics make up a small fraction of all adolescent health clinics, but in contrast to the general lack of male participation in traditional health settings, school-based clinics have demonstrated that young men will use health care services in schools. Of the more than fifty thousand students served by school-based clinics in 1987, nearly four in ten were male.[94]

It takes a village to raise a child, and it takes a village to shape a young father. Schools cannot be the only institution held accountable for young male behavior.

We need a *community* curriculum in parenting education. As suggested in Chapter Four, high school graduation should require that students take a parenting/family issues course from the school, if necessary, but preferably through a community organization—a church, the YMCA, Planned Parenthood, a public-service oriented corporation.

Theoretically, such a choice/voucher approach would not only be less expensive than offering the course only in the schools, but also avoid placing the school in the position of dictating any kind of family values. Indeed, for many young men and women, a church may be a better site than a school for a family-life or sex-education course. Some parents complain that school sex-education programs are too neutral, according to Patrick Welsh, a high school teacher in Alexandria, Virginia, who writes frequently for the *Washington Post*. As one parent told him, schools "seem to be trying too hard not to offend anyone. They are uptight about talking values, but to me 'value free' means valueless." One teenage boy told him that in sex education in his school, "there isn't much discussion. The teacher

Richard Louv

was afraid to say something wrong or get sued." Welsh
writes, "Curiously, teenagers find the church-run programs
more honest and useful than those run by the public
schools."[95]

After I first presented the idea of a required parenting
education course, taught through a community curriculum,
in my newspaper column, I received a number of letters,
but the most interesting comments came from a class of
seniors at Torrey Pines High School, in Del Mar, California.
The teenagers are enrolled in an elective class in child development. The teacher had read my piece to the class and
asked her students to respond. Sixteen of them liked the
proposal, seven did not, and six were ambivalent. Here are
some of the teenagers' comments. First, the cons.

"Sure, you can teach someone to take care of (his or
her) kids physically . . . but when it comes down to it,
parenting is learned by experience."

"California's shrinking budget is the biggest factor that
will eradicate your idea. As a student, I feel the impact of
the budget crisis as I sit in overcrowded classrooms taught
by overworked teachers."

"To be honest, it would burn kids out."

"When a student is in an unwanted course, they're going
to distract the people who want to be there."

"The only reason that I am enrolled in child development is because I have to take a technical art to graduate.
It was either this or wood shop, so I took this. To me,
child development is a waste of time. . . . There are many
people out there like me who don't want children. Why
should we have to deal with something that we don't care
about?"

Now, the pros.

"There are too many teenage pregnancies and young
mothers who have no idea how to raise children."

"A great idea. . . . Making it a college requirement, or a high school graduation requirement, would be an excellent way to make sure that tomorrow's parents are aware and knowledgeable."

"If the parents know their kids are going to get in the water, shouldn't they at least teach them how to swim?"

"I am taking child development at school, and the only reason I took it was because it would be easy. . . . But I have learned so much. Many people don't realize that babies are so complex and so individual from other babies."

"In my current child-development class, we have a total of two boys and forty girls. There need to be more boys. Most guys have no idea of how to raise a child."

One teenager wrote that taking child development had already helped her as a baby-sitter: "Children are just not a priority in this country, no matter what people and politicians say. Even though I feel this way, I certainly don't want to give up hope. . . . Unless we learn otherwise, we are bound to make the same mistakes our parents did. The only problem I see with your idea is getting it passed. People are not too willing to change."

"I have been extremely against having kids myself, and I didn't think I would get much from a class like this. I don't want to have a child because I might grow up and work like my father, who is only home usually one day a month. Because of this, my mother is constantly in a bad mood. . . . My mother takes her sadness and loneliness out on me, and I wouldn't want to put my child through that. I think, however, if I did have a child, I would want to be educated on how to bring him/her up. I totally agree that the course should be widely available so abused children could get help before they inflict this pain on their own children."

All of these comments came from girls. The words of

these teenagers, and the lack of young male voices among them, speak clearly about our need to create a community curriculum in parenting. Education must explore the deeper dimensions of fatherhood; it must emphasize the rewards, to the society, to the child, of good parenting. The school and the community and media must say to young males: Here is the payoff—as a carpenter, you build houses; as a good carpenter your houses stand and deliver long into the future. So it is with fatherhood.

In the courts and at the state and federal levels, we need new policies that encourage fatherlove.

• Marriage must be encouraged. Today, dissolving either a business contract or a business-partner relationship is much more difficult in the United States than dissolving a marriage. No other contract may be breached as easily. Our laws should discourage separation by creating a braking mechanism, a waiting period of nine months for all divorces to become final. (Another possibility: a waiting period before people get married.) The Public Policy Institute, an offshoot of the Democratic Leadership Council, the centrist political organization Bill Clinton helped form in the 1980s, suggests a "children first" principle should govern all divorces involving children. The judge's main task would be to piece together "the best possible package to meet the needs of the children and their physical guardian." Until the welfare of the children was adequately secured, there would be no question or debate about marital property.

• As it encourages fatherlove, society must practice tough fatherlove on abusive fathers and husbands. A task force on domestic violence in San Diego, for example, recommends that people who beat their spouses be jailed for at least ninety-six hours and have to register with authorities, much as sex offenders must do now. "This community can no longer live in denial," said Dr. Nancy Montalvo, a school superintendent who chaired the panel. She decried the lack of attention paid to domestic violence that finds the nation with "two thousand animal shelters and only eight hundred battered women's shelters." (Between 1986 and 1992, the number of domestic violence cases reported to San Diego police jumped from 4,976 incidents to nearly 12,000.) Sending a tough message to abusive fathers is one way to communicate to men what society will not tolerate and let good fathers know that society values them.[96]

• New welfare policies should be designed to encourage fatherhood. One theory gaining currency is the elimination of Aid to Families with Dependent Children (the nation's largest welfare program, created fifty-seven years ago to support widowed women and their children) and the replacement of it with a system to support families—including fathers. Current AFDC rules prevent a woman from receiving full benefits if the father is at home, has an employment record, or works more than a hundred hours a month. In Wisconsin, welfare reform is newly wedded to the philosophy that marriage remains the most dependable escape route from welfare dependency. Under the 1992 Parental and Family Responsibility Initiative, a five-year pilot project, the state allows first-time teen mothers to collect welfare even if they marry their baby's father; it also lets the teenage couples earn more money from working without losing their welfare benefits. (Among other changes, the Wisconsin initiative reduces welfare benefits for parents who have a second child, offers no increase for a third child, and requires young parents to take parenting classes).

Some critics view this approach as discriminatory toward single women; others say it will simply create bad or abusive marriages. As states experiment with bringing the father back into the equation, problems are bound to emerge. But at least a new debate has begun.

• Child-support laws and collection techniques must be toughened, particularly toward affluent fathers. To help assure that fathers pay their child support, the Social Security number of both parents should appear on a child's birth certificate. From the time of the child's birth, absent parents should be expected to contribute a portion of their income for each child; payments should be collected by employers (just as Social Security taxes are today) and sent to the federal government, which would then send the money directly to the custodial parent. Failure to pay would be comparable to tax evasion.

In 1992 Representative Thomas J. Downey, a liberal Long Island Democrat, and Representative Henry J. Hyde, a staunchly conservative Illinois Republican, proposed that the Internal Revenue Service take over all collection duties, but in addition, they recommended that should the IRS fail to collect from the absent father, the federal government make a minimum payment of two thousand dollars a year for a mother with one child; maximum payment per family would be four thousand dollars. The proposal would also create 300,000 new public service jobs to give unemployed fathers a way to make their payments. (Several states now require fathers to join job-search programs: In Grand Rapids, Michigan, a program found jobs for 432 of 1,077 men. As a result, child-support payments jumped by more than 300 percent in eight months.[97]) Downey estimated that his plan could increase the child-support payments collected from the current eleven billion to thirty-five billion dollars a year; poverty and the number of women and children on welfare would likely be decreased. Downey and Hyde estimated that the proposal would cost five billion to ten billion dollars a year. Hyde, the conservative, said of the plan, "The social costs of the current system can't be calculated. We've seen some of it in riots, in lives wasted from the moment they're conceived."[98]

Such an unlikely alliance between a liberal and a conservative offers hope that a new and more sensible family policy is on the way and that it will likely take into account the hardships of motherhood—but also the economic realities of fatherhood.

"If the recent convergence on family policy means anything, it should mean redoubled efforts to devise welfare and tax policies that encourage the formation and retention of stable family units," writes Charles Donovan, executive staff director of the Washington-based Family Research Council. "For liberals this will mean abandoning the vitriolic attacks on marriage and family favored by many within their ranks. For conservatives it will mean a willingness to rely less on sink-or-swim alternatives and to experiment with ideas that risk short-term costs for long-term gains. But restoring the cultural and legal norm of the marital family is a prize worth the effort."[99]

We must bring fatherlove home. We must challenge our attitudes about fatherhood within our own family systems. For example, when a man does take family leave or decide to be a part- or full-time at-home dad, he may encounter subtle or not-so-subtle messages from his in-laws, such as: Aren't you working? Don't you have a job yet? A mother can also communicate conflicting messages about the father's involvement. Most women (and men) grew up being told that child-rearing was primarily a woman's job. Such a sense of responsibility is difficult to share, particularly if the man is also sending out mixed messages; he may say he wants to do more at home, but he may also find his wife's subtle resistance a useful excuse to dodge his own responsibilities.

With as much power as men still have in our culture, we can hardly think of ourselves as victims. A child who has been abandoned by a father does not care that institutions or families have resisted fatherhood. The child only knows that the father is gone. Here is the bottom line: The causes of fatherlessness and the primary responsibility for creating and spreading fatherlove do not rest on the shoulders of women, but in the hands of men. That responsibility must be both political and personal. As one mother says, "We're not going to see much political progress until a lot more fathers are as likely as mothers to get up in the middle of the night when a child cries."

Fatherlove is like any kind of love. It's impossible to define, but we know it when we feel it. No single formula can capture it, and no single list of approaches can fully describe what must be done to encourage it. But here are a few specific things that we, as individuals, can do to create and promote fatherlove in our nation, our institutions, and in our everyday life:

• Acknowledge the worth of fatherhood. Say to ourselves and to others: *I am a father and I am proud of it.* Unless this is made clear, no other pronouncements or programs will help.

• In every way possible, reconnect fatherhood and manhood.

• View fatherhood as multidimensional; see it as the fullness of masculinity, as a profound and endless adventure.

- Communicate openly about the double messages and unspoken power disputes between men and women at home, at work, and in the community.
- Whether married or never married, divorced or separated, view parenting as an equal partnership between the mother and the father.
- Advocate fatherlove. Even if a man is not a father, even if his children are grown or gone, he can express fatherlove. Promote, in every possible way, the power of fatherlove—for instance, the relationship between a father's nurturing and the development of empathy in his children. And spread the word about the benefits men gain by being good fathers.
- Build the village. Take fatherlove into our communities, into our workplaces, into our places of worship.
- Mentor or coach younger fathers and young men. Become a grandfatherman.
- Fight negative stereotypes of fathers, particularly in the media; and fight family stereotypes that assume parenting is mothers' work only.
- Challenge attitudes that exclude or excuse men from participating in the care and education of our children.
- Create new ways, and revive old ones, for men to talk with each other about fathering—and also to talk with mothers about parenting.
- Fight gender double standards in parenting education; create school and community curricula that, as early as possible in children's lives, teach and demonstrate the value of fathers.
- Honor work, but not at the expense of children. Integrate children into the world of work; integrate men into the world of children.
- Scrutinize the policies of institutions toward fathers, as well as the language used to describe family issues. For

example, in the workplace, support and promote family leave for mothers *and* fathers.

• Fight to make our workplaces more family-friendly.

• Practice personal tough love on fathers: Tell abusive or abandoning dads what you think of their behavior. This is especially effective when men communicate their opinions to other men.

• Be a political fatherman. In order to make real change happen, our country needs far more than a legislative package. We need a movement led by men and women in full partnership. Like the feminist movement, a family movement must be both personal and political. It must be a grass roots movement; it must enlist nonparents in the cause; it must mobilize the churches; it must target company cultures; it must launch parent voter-registration drives; it must utilize ballot initiatives; it must create self-help and consciousness-raising groups; and, in addition to the many courageous women now working for change, it must identify male leaders by challenging their manhood. Real men fight for all our children.

Government alone cannot force men to be good fathers, nor can business, nor community, nor even a family movement. Ultimately, fatherlove is personal. The degree to which fatherhood is valued by our culture depends fundamentally on the stories men tell each other about fathering, and on the stories we tell our children. And we must leave some room for magic.

I began this book with a story about my younger son; I end it with one about my older son.

As we left the dock, we felt the cool air coming up from the water. Fishing air feels and smells like no other air. It cools your face and gets in under your shirt, and everything is left behind—all work, all worries, all the meaningless static of the city.

Jason was seven at the time. Watching his hands, I remembered how my father's hands could whip a lure out and make it curve in the air.

"Remember last time?" asked Jason as he let his line out behind us.

I did. The last time we had gone fishing at this lake, we had nearly reached the mystery valley, as we called it, at dusk. We could see the violet hills and the green pastures and the cattle and the little river running through the willows. "The closer we get, the farther away it seems," I had said to Jason. His eyes had grown wide. The light had been red and fading, and the valley seemed to recede before us. We had turned back.

"I'd like to go to the mystery valley this time," said Jason.

Suddenly five or six of what looked like giant, aggressive water bugs came howling across the waves. Jet skis. We slowly fished our way away toward the mystery valley.

Then Jason got a strike. He strained at the reel. "Keep reeling, you can do it," I said. And he did. He brought the bass into the boat, and it seemed to grow before our eyes. Jason was breathing hard. So was I.

The wind was coming up. We had drifted into the weeds. I tried to start the engine, but it snagged on something, made a choking noise and stopped. I leaned over the back of the boat and remembered, in my father's voice, *the cotter pin.* I tried to replace it with some of the wire holding the engine to the boat. It didn't work.

I swore at the engine and then for some reason recalled my favorite memory of my father—reaching out from the boat to grab a branch, then going overboard, rod and glasses suspended in the air as he sank in slow motion beneath the surface. I carry this home movie in my heart ... how he laughed, later, and stripped off his wet clothes and ran through the trees on a little island, making a Tarzan yell, showing off for my mother. I remembered her laughing.

The engine was shot. We'd have to row back. I pushed us off and tried the oars, but the old pins were bent. So I moved to the bow of the boat. Jason handed me one of the oars, and I tried to paddle out into the rising wind. "Well, we're not going to make it," I said, half to myself. We beached the boat and walked around a bend to see if there were any boats along the shore.

"What about rattlesnakes?" said Jason.

"Stay right behind me. I'm looking. . . ."

"Dad."

"What?" I was squinting across the lake. Two boats were out there in the distance, not moving. Worm fishing. "Dad." The boats were out of earshot.

"Somebody's following us."

I looked behind us. The brush moved slightly in the wind.

"Really, Dad. I've been feeling somebody watching us." He looked a little shivery.

"No, Jase, nobody's following us. That's just your sea legs. Getting on land after being in the boat can make you feel that way."

He didn't look convinced.

We returned to the boat. Jason sat on a rock with his chin in his hand, eating a rice cake. We looked out over the lake, which right then seemed as wide and formidable as the Pacific. We watched the jet skis off in the distance with their spouts shooting up and drifting into the wind. They looked oddly beautiful now, like a pod of whales. Finally, a boat came by close enough for us to flag it down.

It was one of those supercharged boats, with plenty of strength to tow us back.

Once hooked up, it took a long time to get back to the dock.

I thought about my father again, how he had finally achieved his dream of living on a lake. But by then, before he was gone, he had lost interest in dreams or fishing. He had quit walking down to the water.

Fumes from the tow boat flowed past us. Jason looked a little green and sleepy. Using the flotation cushions, I made a bed for him on the floor of the boat, just as my father had done for me when we had night fished.

"I don't think I want to fish any more today," Jason said. He looked as if he was going to cry. Low blood sugar, maybe. I changed the subject. "How did it feel to catch the bass? Did your knees shake? My knees shake sometimes when I—"

He blurted out, "Wrong. It felt . . . wrong."

Wrong? The morality of seven-year-olds is always startling, confrontal, clean. I talked to him about the fish we buy at the grocery store and how I didn't believe it was wrong to catch fish if you ate them. He nodded. "How about if we throw the fish back from now on?" He nodded faster.

We were silent for a while.

Then he said he hadn't been very brave.

"Sure you were."

"But I was scared."

"Nobody's brave unless they're scared."

He brightened. "Maybe who was following us was just the water," he said. "You know, just the sound of the waves."

We didn't reach the mystery valley that day. We stopped at a roadside restaurant instead. Jason ordered fried cod fillets.

I figured Jason wouldn't want to go fishing again any-time soon, not after getting scared and having an attack of morality and watching his father flounder around the lake and listening to all those damned jet skis. Then my son announced, with enthusiasm, "Dad, that was the best fishing trip yet. When are we going again?" Pause. "Could you pass the salt?"

Two years passed. I thought he had pretty much forgotten about the valley, but one day he announced that there was one more thing he wanted to do before school started. "Find the mystery valley," he said.

This time, at dawn, we headed straight for the endless arm and the valley at the end. It took a long time to get there, but as we approached, Jason said with awe, "It looks like Africa."

And it did, or a cross between Africa and New Mexico. Above, we could see late summer cumulus clouds, the kind in which you can find the face of anything or anybody you want. The foothills looked like pink sheets plucked up by invisible fingers, and a stream ran between them and out of another century, meandering slow as Sunday morning, through willows and cottonwoods, oozing eventually through a marsh and into the lake.

The water had recently risen to the knees and waists of young trees that had grown up during the drought.

"Look!" said Jason, sitting at the bow of the boat. Ahead, we saw fields of mustard grass, yellow daisies and cattle, and two white egrets standing tall, lifting their feet in slow motion, watching the surface of the water.

Now we moved through the shallows and into the stream, and running the outboard slowly, we glided between the drowning bushes. Minnows shot ahead and to each side. The air closed in. Jason's job was to watch for stumps and hidden obstructions below the surface and to tell his father when the water grew too shallow. He knelt on the front seat and leaned over.

"Dad, a log . . . Dad, an . . . *alligator!*"

He straightened up, eyes wide. He thought, at first, he

had seen a log. "But then the log moved forward real quick and ate a minnow." He said the thing was as long as the boat, or almost as long.

He had probably seen a big catfish or bass, I told him. I explained about the magnification of water, and added, "But then again it could be"—I paused—"the monster of mystery valley."

Jason rolled his eyes. Nine-year-olds do a lot of eye-rolling. But I could tell part of him believed in the possibility and that he was pleased.

When you're seven or eight or even nine, anything is possible in nature.

One of my first memories is of an early morning on the Lake of the Ozarks, looking up at the sky as my father and mother loaded rods and tackle boxes into a boat and seeing the sun rise—a sun so swollen that it seemed to fill a third of the sky. To this day, part of my mind still believes that on certain magical days, the sun is as big as the sky.

Now, Jason and I moved forward, got stuck a couple times, poled out with an oar. And far up the stream, where the air grew silent, we banked the boat and got out. I wanted to see what was in the line of trees; perhaps it was another, deeper channel. So we headed across a mushy field of high weeds, through drifting clouds of green, newly hatched flies. Our feet sank down now, six inches below the surface, then more. . . .

At the edge of the trees was a shallow pool of muddy water where something moved beneath the surface. As we approached, a phalanx of panicked life charged away from us, churning the water. We waded on, beneath the trees, where the light was coming down in a kind of sunfall through the branches, and then we stood, awestruck in the silence. As far as we could see was what appeared to be a field of glowing, green snow. We reached down, both of us, and scooped up fistfuls of duckweed, each plant having the delicacy of miniature clover.

Both of us, I think, stopped breathing for a moment, and we stood there for a long time looking out across that scene, and finally we let out our breath.

After a while we headed back to the brown pool and knelt in the water. "Feel around," I said, moving my hands in the muck below the surface.

"Dad, *yuck.*"

"Really, do it." He did, and I felt something moving, then came up with it in my hand: a squirming, fat bullfrog tadpole.

Back at the stream, Jason, excited and proud, caught one, too.

After a while, I took my rod from the boat and waded along the stream, and Jason fished a few feet from me. As we talked I saw a flash of color and a good-sized bass hit just below the surface. Jason watched his excited father step out to play the fish and then fall into the stream and hoot and holler and hang on to the fish and haul it in. We looked down to see another bigger bass following it in. Then we knelt and looked at the bass I had caught. I held it in the water and stroked its belly then let it go, and it slowly swam away.

I hope that Jason keeps this memory, but you never know. I hope as he and his brother grow older, they leave some room for magic. Perhaps when Jason is my age, part of him will still believe in the monster of mystery valley or that the closer you are to a place, the farther away it can become.

We turned the boat and moved back down the stream. Jason again scouted the shadows in the water, watching for danger, until he could no longer see the bottom and the valley disappeared around a bend.

I want to be a father until the day I die.

Bibliography

Annie E. Casey Foundation, The; Center for the Study of Social Policy. *Kids Count Data Book: State Profiles of Child Well-Being.* Greenwich, Conn.: The Annie E. Casey Foundation; Washington, D.C.: Center for the Study of Social Policy, 1992.

Bly, Robert. *Iron John: A Book about Men.* New York: Vintage Books, a division of Random House, Inc., 1990.

Canfield, Ken R. *The 7 Secrets of Effective Fathers: Becoming the father you want to be.* Wheaton, Illinois: Tyndale House Publishers, Inc., 1992.

Cherlin, Andrew J., and Frank F. Furstenberg, Jr. *The New American Grandparent: A Place in the Family, A Life Apart.* New York: Basic Books Inc., Publishers, 1986.

Coles, Robert. *The Spiritual Life of Children.* Boston: Houghton Mifflin Company, 1990.

Corneau, Guy. *Absent Fathers, Lost Sons: The Search for Masculine Identity.* Boston: Shambhala Publications Inc., 1991.

Erikson, Erik H. *The Life Cycle Completed.* New York: W. W. Norton & Co. Inc., 1982.

Fox, C. Lynn, and Shirley E. Forbing. *Creating Drug-Free Schools and Communities: A Comprehensive Approach.* New York: HarperCollins, 1992.

Franklin, Clyde W., II. *Men & Society.* Chicago: Nelson-Hall Publishers, 1988.

Greif, Geoffrey L. *Single Fathers.* Lexington, Mass.: Lexington Books, a division of D C Heath and Company, 1985.

Hamburg, David A., M.D. *Today's Children: Creating a Future for a Generation in Crisis.* New York: Times Books, a subsidiary of Random House, Inc., 1992.

Heinowitz, Jack. *Pregnant Fathers: How Fathers Can Enjoy and Share the Experiences of Pregnancy and Childbirth.* New York: Prentice Hall Press, 1982.

Jackson, Michael, and Jessica Jackson, edited by Bruce Jackson. *"Your Father's Not Coming Home Anymore."* New York: Ace Books, published by arrangement with the Putnam Publishing Company, 1981.

Keyes, Ralph. *Sons on Fathers.* New York: HarperCollins, 1992.

FatherLove

Levine, Judith. *My Enemy, My Love: Man-Hating and Ambivalence in Women's Lives.* New York: Doubleday, 1992.

Louv, Richard. *Childhood's Future.* New York: Anchor Books, Doubleday, 1990.

National Commission on Children. *Beyond Rhetoric: A New American Agenda for Children and Families.* Washington, D.C.: National Commission on Children (U.S.), and U.S. Government Printing Office, 1991.

Oldenburg, Ray. *The Great Good Place: Cafes, Coffee Shops, Community Centers, Beauty Parlors, General Stores, Bars, Hangouts, and How They Get You Through the Day.* New York: Paragon House Publishers, 1989.

Pruett, Kyle D., M.D. *The Nurturing Father.* New York: Warner Books, Inc., 1988.

Salk, Lee, Dr. *Familyhood: Nurturing the Values That Matter.* New York: Simon & Schuster, 1992.

Secunda, Victoria. *Women and Their Fathers: The Sexual and Romantic Impact of the First Man in Your Life.* New York: Delacorte Press, 1992.

Wallerstein, Judith S.; Blakeslee, Sandra. *Second Chances: Men, Women & Children a Decade After Divorce.* New York: Ticknor & Fields, 1990.

Yablonsky, Lewis, Ph.D. *Fathers & Sons; The Most Challenging of All Family Relationships.* New York: Gardner Press Trade Book Company, 1990.

Notes

[1]Hugh O'Neill, "Sex Cool," *Mothering*, Summer, 1991, pp. 118–119. Adapted and reprinted in *Mothering* w/permission from *Daddy Cool*, © 1988 by Hugh O'Neill. (New York: Warner Books, Inc.)

[2]Armin A. Brott, "Not All Men Are Sly Foxes," *Newsweek*, June 1, 1992, pp. 14–15.

[3]Robert Mannis, "Husbandry," *The Utne Reader*, May/June 1991, pp. 70–71.

[4]David Blankenhorn, "The Vanishing Father," *Atlanta Journal—Atlanta Constitution*, November 4, 1990, p. G–1.

[5]Blankenhorn, "The Vanishing Father," p. G–1.

[6]Massachusetts Mutual Life Insurance is one of the country's leading mutual insurers. MassMutual has been a

pioneer in researching America's family values since 1988.

[7]"The Revolution in Family Life," *The Futurist,* Sept/Oct. 1990, pp. 53–54.

[8]Tamar Lewin, "Father's Vanishing Act Called Common Drama," *New York Times,* June 4, 1990, p. A–18.

[9]Jeanne Ambrose, "A Solo Decision," *Grand Rapids Press,* June 24, 1992, p. D–1.

[10]Myron Magnet, "The American Family, 1992," *Fortune,* August 10, 1992, p. 43, and Paul Taylor, " 'Two Faces of Fatherhood': Dads Become More Domesticated, More Distant," *Washington Post,* June 16, 1991, p. A–1, © 1991, *The Washington Post.* Reprinted with permission.

[11]Remarks by Louis W. Sullivan, M.D., at the Institute for American Values Council on Families in America, New York City, January 9, 1992.

[12]Nina J. Easton, "Life Without Father," *Los Angeles Times Magazine,* June 14, 1992, p. 15.

[13]Charles Donovan, "Why Children Need Both Their Parents," *San Diego Union-Tribune,* August 2, 1992, p. C–4.

[14]Taylor, "Two Faces of Fatherhood," p. A–1.

[15]Magnet, "The American Family, 1992," p. 44.

[16]Magnet, "The American Family, 1992," p. 44.

FatherLove

[17]John Leo, "A Pox on Dan and Murphy," *U.S. News & World Report,* June 1, 1992, p. 19.

[18]Judy Mann, "Murphy, Where's My Pa?" *Washington Post,* May 15, 1992, p. E–3.

[19]Magnet, "The American Family, 1992," p. 44.

[20]Magnet, "The American Family, 1992," p. 44.

[21]Magnet, "The American Family, 1992," p. 44.

[22]Associated Press, "Survey Finds 46% Fear for Their Jobs," *San Diego Union-Tribune,* May 5, 1992, p. A–12.

[23]Blayne Cutler, "Rock-A-Buy-Baby," *American Demographics,* January 1990, pp. 37–39.

[24]Janice Castro, "Work Ethic—In Spades," *Time,* February 17, 1992, p. 57.

[25]Easton, "Life Without Father," p. 15.

[26]Ken Clatterbaugh, "Are Men Still the Breadwinners?" *The Utne Reader,* May/June 1991, pp. 82–83.

[27]Barbara Ehrenreich, "Angry Young Men," *The Utne Reader,* May/June 1991, pp. 78–80. Excerpted in *The Utne Reader* with permission from *New York Woman,* September 1989. Copyright 1989 by *New York Woman* magazine.

[28]John Byrne Barry, "Balancing Fatherhood and Career," *Mothering,* Spring 1989, pp. 17–23.

[29]Aaron Latham, "Fathering the Nest," *M*, May 1992, pp. 66–75.

[30]Teresa Opheim, "Potential Papas Beware," *The Utne Reader*, July/August 1991, pp. 26–27.

[31]Lisa Schroepfer, "Dad: New & Improved," *American Health*, June 1991, p. 64. © American Health Partners 1991.

[32]Latham, "Fathering the Nest," pp. 66–75.

[33]Sue Shellenbarger, "Employers Set Rules for Doing Homework," *Wall Street Journal*, August 16, 1991, p. B–1.

[34]Shellenbarger, "Employers Set Rules for Doing Homework," p. B–1.

[35]Sue Shellenbarger, "Work & Family," *Wall Street Journal*, May 27, 1992, p. B–1.

[36]Latham, "Fathering the Nest," pp. 66–75.

[37]David Blankenhorn, Letter to the Editor, published in *USA Today*, April 13, 1992.

[38]Taylor, "Two Faces of Fatherhood," p. A–1.

[39]Schroepfer, "Dad: New & Improved," p. 64.

[40]Marilyn Elias, "Dad's Role Crucial to Caring Kids," *USA Today*, May 30, 1990, p. 1–A.

[41]Daniel Goleman, "Studies on Development of Empathy

Challenge Some Old Assumptions," *New York Times*, July 12, 1990, p. B–8.

[42]"The New Father: Part Reality, Part Media Hype, Says Psychologist." Release from *Stanford News*, February 22, 1989.

[43]Paul Ciotti, "How Fathers Figure," *Los Angeles Times Magazine*, June 18, 1989, p. 10.

[44]Elvira Valenzuela Crocker, "Today, a Fitting Recipe for Fathers of Latina Daughters," *San Diego Union-Tribune*, June 21, 1992, p. C–8.

[45]Sharon Griffin, "A Father's Example: A Black Woman Learns to Believe in Herself," *Providence Sunday Journal*, June 21, 1987, p. C–1.

[46]Samuel Osherson, "Finding our Fathers," *The Utne Reader*, April/May 1986, pp. 36–42.

[47]Thom R. McFarland, "Disposable Daddies," *Mothering*, Fall 1991, pp. 117–19.

[48]Taylor, "Two Faces of Fatherhood," p. A–1.

[49]Taylor, "Two Faces of Fatherhood," p. A–1.

[50]Schroepfer, "Dad: New & Improved," p. 64.

[51]Schroepfer, "Dad: New & Improved," p. 64.

[52]Peter J. Dorsen, "Fathering: A Matter of Enlightenment," *Mothering*, Spring 1989, pp. 24–27.

[53]Dorsen, "Fathering: A Matter of Enlightenment," pp. 24–27.

[54]Randall Beach, "Househusbands," *The Utne Reader*, March/April 1990, pp. 79–82.

[55]Beach, "Househusbands," pp. 79–82.

[56]Latham, "Fathering the Nest," pp. 66–75.

[57]"The New Father: Part Reality, Part Media Hype, Says Psychologist." Release from *Stanford News*.

[58]Schroepfer, "Dad: New & Improved," p. 64.

[59]Schroepfer, "Dad: New & Improved," p. 64.

[60]Latham, "Fathering the Nest," pp. 66–75.

[61]Latham, "Fathering the Nest," pp. 66–75.

[62]Emily Ashton and Stella Bugbee, eds., "After All These Years, Kids Still See Trap in Sex Roles," *Dallas Times Herald*, March 20, 1991.

[63]Dave Barry, "A Beginner's Guide to Housework (or Everything You Guys Always Wanted to Know About Dirty Toilets)," *The Utne Reader*, March/April 1990, p. 87.

[64]Debbie Taylor, "Life Sentence: The Politics of Housework," *New Internationalist*, March 1988, pp. 4–6.

[65]Taylor, "Life Sentence: The Politics of Housework," pp. 4–6.

[66] Arlie Hochschild, "The Second Shift: Employed Women Are Putting in Another Day of Work at Home," *The Utne Reader*, March/April 1990, pp. 66–73.

[67] John P. Robinson, "The Hard Facts About Hard Work," *The Utne Reader*, March/April 1990, p. 70.

[68] Sue Shellenbarger, "Two-Earner Families May Produce Sexist Sons," *Wall Street Journal*, July 15, 1991, p. B–1.

[69] Taylor, "Two Faces of Fatherhood, p. A–1.

[70] Edward F. Sigler and Elizabeth P. Gilman, "An Agenda for the 1990's: Supporting Families," from D. Blankenhorn, S. Bayme, and J.B. Elshtain, eds., *Rebuilding the Nest: A New Commitment to the American Family*. (Milwaukee: Family Service America, 1990), p. 239.

[71] Ray Oldenburg, *The Great Good Place* (New York: Paragon House, 1989), p. 246.

[72] Larry Letich, "Do You Know Who Your Friends Are?" *The Utne Reader*, May/June 1991, pp. 85–87.

[73] Hank Whittemore, "Security Dads," *Parade*, September 27, 1992, pp. 20–22. Reprinted with permission from *Parade*, © 1992.

[74] Sanford M. Dornbusch et al., "Single Parents, Extended Households and the Control of Adolescents," *Child Development* 56 (1985): 326–41.

[75] Crocker, "Today, a Fitting Recipe for Fathers of Latina Daughters," p. C–8.

[76]John McKnight, "Are Social Service Agencies the Enemy of Community?" *The Utne Reader*, July/August 1992, pp. 88–90.

[77]Paul Leinberger and Bruce Tucker, "The Boomers' Search for Community," *The Utne Reader*, July/August 1992, pp. 86–88.

[78]Osherson, "Finding our Fathers," pp. 36–42.

[79]Osherson, "Finding our Fathers," pp. 36–42.

[80]Osherson, "Finding our Fathers," pp. 36–42.

[81]Kathleen Marie Philbin, "The Transmission of Religiosity from Parents to Their Young Adult Children," Dissertation Abstrs International, Volume 49/07–B, (1988): p. 2892.

[82]David Heller, "The Children's God; the Gods Must Be Changing—to Meet the Emotional Needs of Growing Children," *Psychology Today*, December 1985, p. 22.

[83]Guy Corneau, *Absent Fathers, Lost Sons* (Shambhala: Boston, 1991), p. 181.

[84]Corneau, p. 181.

[85]Corneau, pp. 145, 146

[86]Corneau, pp. 148, 149.

[87]Kyle D. Pruett, M.D., *The Nurturing Father* (New York: Warner Books, Inc. 1988), p. 27.

[88]Easton, "Life Without Father," p. 15.

[89]Gregory Max Vogt, Ph.D., and Stephen T. Sirridge, Ph.D., *Like Son, Like Father: Healing the Father-Son Wound in Men's Lives.* (NY: Plenum Press, 1991), p. 81.

[90]Andrew Kimbrall, "A Time for Men to Pull Together," *The Utne Reader*, May/June 1991, pp. 66–74.

[91]Sophfronia Scott Gregory, "Teaching Young Fathers the Ropes," *Time*, August 10, 1992, p. 49.

[92]Barbara Kantrowitz, "Kids and Contraceptives," *Newsweek*, February 16, 1987, p. 60.

[93]Richard Stengel, "The Missing-Father Myth," *Time*, December 9, 1985, p. 90.

[94]"What About the Boys? Teenage Pregnancy Prevention Strategies." (Publication of the Adolescent Pregnancy Prevention Clearinghouse, Children's Defense Fund, August 1988.)

[95]Patrick Welsh, "Sex, Silence and Family Hypocrisy; When Teens and Parents Don't Talk, Kids Get the Wrong Message," *Washington Post*, June 2, 1991, p. D–1.

[96]Dwight Daniels, "Blue-ribbon Panel Urges Jailing of Spouse Beaters," *San Diego Union-Tribune*, May 14, 1992, p. B–2.

[97]Steven Waldman, "Seeking New Solutions," *Newsweek*, May 4, 1992, p. 49.

[98]Jason DeParle, "Radical Overhaul Proposed in System of Child Support," *The New York Times*, May 13, 1992, p. A–16.

[99]Donovan, "Why Children Need Both Their Parents," p. C–4.

EAST ORANGE PUBLIC LIBRARY
FatherLove : what we need, what we seek
306.87 L894 / Louv, Richard.

3 2665 0011 5891 6

306.87 L894 cop.1 $21.00

Louv, Richard.

FatherLove

There is a penalty for removing either the book
card or the control card from this pocket.
EAST ORANGE PUBLIC LIBRARY
21 So. Arlington
Branches—Ampere, 39 Ampere Plaza—Franklin, 192 Dodd Street
Elmwood, 317 South Clinton Street
EAST ORANGE, NEW JERSEY